In My Calm Era

90 Days to Organize Your Emotions, Stress Less, & Connect Back to You

HARPER
Celebrate

In My Calm Era

Published by Harper Celebrate, an imprint of HarperCollins Focus LLC.

Any internet addresses (websites, blogs, etc.) in this book are offered as a resource. They are not intended in any way to be or imply an endorsement by HarperCollins Focus LLC, nor does HarperCollins Focus LLC vouch for the content of these sites for the life of this book.

Note: Readers agree and acknowledge that this book does not provide medical advice or mental health advice in any way. Always seek the advice of your own medical provider and/or mental health provider regarding any questions or concerns you have about your specific health.

Cover design by Susanna Chapman

Art direction by Tiffany Forrester

Interior design by Lauren Clulow

ISBN 978-1-4002-5244-2 (HC)
ISBN 978-1-4002-5245-9 (epub)

Printed in Malaysia

25 26 27 28 29 PJM 5 4 3 2 1

Contents

Introduction

I f you picked up a book with the word *calm* in the title, chances are you're not feeling a whole lot of it. You're not alone. Stress, anxiety, and burnout are issues everyone experiences at some point. If anyone tells you otherwise, they're either lying or the luckiest person on earth and should probably play the lotto.

Here's the deal: In some seasons of life, just getting through the day can feel brutal. Maybe you're overwhelmed at school or work, responsible for little ones, worried about a loved one, or generally unsure what comes next. We. Are. Tired.

You are doing hard things. We have no doubt your fears, worries, anxiety, and panic are well-earned. You're out there doing your best, and we first want to celebrate that. But that daily pit in your stomach? The racing thoughts and shortness of breath? Friend, you know you can't keep going like that forever. And the good news is you really don't have to. You don't have to live your life in an anxious, sleepless era, spiraling from one chaotic thought to another. So if you're ready to break the cycle of panic and find a new era of calm, you're in the right place.

Maybe you're coming to these pages because anxiety is new to you, or maybe this is something you've struggled with your whole life. Over the course of ninety days, you're going to learn how to honor your emotions, whatever they may be, discover how to soften the panic and negativity, and reclaim more joy and peace in your life. Sounds pretty good, right?

Consider this book a gift to yourself. And for ninety days, dedicate time to your wellness. Doing so will leave you feeling more confident, joyous, and calm than you are today.

IN THIS BOOK, YOU'LL:

❀ **Reconnect with your breath and body.** Both your breath and your body tell the story of your emotions, but it takes practice to discern them. In this journey, you'll get to know the physical symptoms you feel when you're anxious or stressed and how to spot them before you spiral. You'll also practice techniques to help calm and regulate your nervous system when you're feeling overwhelmed. This will help you regulate your racing mind and focus on the present, and on what is true and real about your situation.

❀ **Practice, practice, practice.** Treat this book like a training program for your anxious mind. Each day, spend time completing activities that encourage you to dive deep, change your thinking, adjust your routine, and let go of fear.

❀ **Be honest about your feelings and experiences.** We encourage you to grab a journal or use a note-taking app to become vulnerable about the emotions you're feeling and what you're learning about yourself. After all, no one will see it but you! (Well, unless you have a terrible hiding place for your journal, but that's on you!)

❀ **Get to know yourself better.** Completing the prompts and activities will allow you to get to the heart of what you're feeling and to the core of who you are. You'll spend time with yourself every day, which isn't always a priority (or even particularly comfortable) when you're feeling stressed or anxious. You'll gather new information about yourself, and in doing so you'll be able to speak truth over your circumstances.

❀ **Gain confidence in yourself.** You'll practice letting go of your stress and anxiety, replacing them with positivity and calm. As you get comfortable with the activities and prompts, you'll gain confidence in yourself.

❀ **Enter your calm era.** Need we say more? When all is said and done, you'll have a new access to calm. You will be someone who can spot when you're getting anxious or stressed, allowing you to address the problem and find your peace even in tough situations.

THIS BOOK PAIRS WELL WITH:

✎ **A journal and something to write with.** Or use a note-taking app on your phone, or anyplace you like to store your thoughts. There will be many moments in the next ninety days when you'll be asked to reflect on the day's topic or complete an activity. Writing is a helpful processing tool, and it can be rewarding to look at the first pages of this journal and compare who you are today as you start the journey with who you become and how you feel at the end of it.

♥ **An open mind.** Some of these activities might feel different and maybe even a little silly. But try to stay open to new experiences. We encourage you to approach each day with an open mind and open heart, committing to the activities without placing any judgment on yourself.

That's it! There's no wrong way to complete these ninety days—you simply need to start. So carve out a few minutes each day, and let's usher in a new era of you.

SEE YOU ON THE OTHER SIDE, FRIEND!

Let It Go

S tress isn't something that happens only in your mind. It is also deeply felt in your body. Your breath becomes rapid, your shoulders creep up to your ears, you clench your jaw, your head throbs. It's easy to tell yourself that it doesn't get any better and it's normal to feel this way. Here's the truth: It's common, but it's not normal.

You have the power to stop stress in its tracks, and sometimes the gentlest way to practice this is by addressing the physical symptoms first. What's stressing you will eventually need to be addressed (more on that later), but a simple way to manage stress is to physically let it go.

Because you are in control of your body, you have at least some agency over the stress that manifests within it. Whether you've been waking up feeling stressed (been there!) or find that you can't relax at the end of the day because your mind is abuzz, spending time understanding where stress is manifesting in your body can change the game when it comes to your stress management.

SHAKE IT OUT

Let's uncover where you're holding your tension. Can't pinpoint it? No worries (that would be counterproductive)! Try shaking out your body. This may feel silly, but go with it. Stand in a neutral position and take some breaths to ground yourself. Then shake one part of your body at a time. Start with your fingers and toes, then your arms, your legs, your hips, your shoulders, and even your head. Finish with a deep breath. Pay attention to where you feel tight or inflexible, and give extra care to these areas.

---- **AFFIRMATION** ----

I have control over my body. ✦ I can release the tension ✦ I'm feeling.

DAY 2

Find Your Breath

E xperiencing stress feels like running a race without knowing where the finish line is. You started this race feeling confident, but with every hill you climb, doubts creep in. *Am I going the right way? Do I have it in me to keep moving forward? Am I wearing the right shoes? Uh-oh, I* am *wearing the wrong shoes.*

Feel familiar? When you set out each morning trying to keep pace with everyone around you, it's easy to disconnect from your purpose. Have you lost sight of why you started the race? That's a good sign it's time to take a moment to yourself to walk away and catch your breath. Or maybe you need to fully lie down and recuperate. There's no point in racing ahead in your day if you've lost track of where you're going. So untie those shoelaces and take a beat.

It sounds too simple to be true, but one of the keys to finding your calm is connecting back to one of the things that comes most naturally to you: breathing. Only from this place of calm can you begin to evaluate whether you're headed in the direction you desire.

I breathe in calm, I breathe out stress.

BOX BREATHE

Put your hand over your heart. Breathe in for four counts, hold for four, breathe out for four, hold for four. This is called box breathing,[1] and it helps you reconnect with your breath when you're feeling stressed or anxious. Try to send your breath down into your belly, rather than into your chest. Return to this deep form of breathing whenever you need to re-center yourself.

MIND

DAY 3

Sit in Stillness

How often are you still? Like, *genuinely* still? When you do take a break, do you feel the urge to check your email or fill your time with chores instead? When you're experiencing anxiety and stress, stillness can feel impossible to achieve. Plus, that to-do list isn't going to take care of itself. Not a moment to lose, right?

Wrong.

We live in a world that values forward motion and productivity, so it's important to reframe how you think about taking a quiet moment for yourself. Stillness is far from unproductive. In fact, it's one of the most productive things you can do. Pausing to clear your mind is kind of like performing a factory reset on your brain. After you do it, you'll be operating at a greater level and capacity than you were before.

Whenever you feel like you can't possibly find five minutes to yourself, this is a red flag! *Step away from the task list, people!* Take the time to clear your head. Only then will you have space for hope. That's well worth a few minutes of stillness, don't you think?

TAKE A MOMENT TO MEDITATE

Set a timer at either the start or end of your day—or both. Find a comfortable place to sit or lie down with good posture and alignment. Once you're comfortable, close your eyes and focus on your breath. Breathe in, breathe out. Don't be discouraged if your mind wanders. Instead, be proud for noticing when it does, then return your focus to your breath. Continue through your allotted time, and simply notice the thoughts that come up. Make sure to return to this practice. It gets easier every time, we promise!

—————— AFFIRMATION ——————

I can hit ✦ pause and set aside ✦ time to clear ✦ my mind.

MIND

DAY 4

Take It All In

H ave you ever watched a toddler experience a new place for the first time? Their eyes grow wide, and they can't decide which way to look. They're on the hunt for the best toy, and they barrel ahead, even if they don't quite have the motor skills. They simply want to be in this world wholeheartedly. They're curious about colors, textures, and people and allow themselves to express their feelings: fear, joy, excitement. All of it is acceptable!

As we get older, fewer and fewer experiences stir wonder in us. The more we experience, the less surprise we feel. That's just the nature of growing older. It thus becomes more and more important to ask: How can we get back to that childlike wonder? How can we usher in curiosity in place of anxiety?

When you practice greeting difficult tasks with a toddler-like anticipation, you take the pressure off. Learning to deprioritize your expectations and practice openness is a true emotional superpower. Accepting that you don't know everything about a situation, place, or person gives you the chance to be surprised and delighted.

WONDER AND WANDER

Start or end your day with a technology-free Wonder Walk. As you walk around your neighborhood or a nearby park, take this time to become curious about the little things you pass by every day. When you experience your surroundings through a lens of wonder, you give yourself the opportunity to view the world positively rather than from a deficit. Take note of anything that delights you, and note your ability to shift your emotions. Practicing curiosity in low-stakes moments will better equip you to embrace curiosity in high-stakes ones.

---- **AFFIRMATION** ----

I will be curious in hard times and look for beauty to center myself.

DAY 5

Check Your Compass

If you were sending someone you love on a long hike or camping trip, there are a few things you would pack to be sure their journey was smooth and safe. You'd check their backpack for snacks and supplies so they wouldn't be hungry, make sure the first aid kit was stocked in case of emergency, and double-check that they had a way to navigate themselves to their destination.

Even for the directionally challenged among us (hi, it's me), your internal compass will orient you when you're feeling lost, boost your confidence that you're headed in the right direction, or help you change course if the path ahead no longer suits you. You can use your internal compass to look not only forward to what comes next but also back at the direction from which you came. It's important, then, to check your compass periodically to be sure you're in tune with where you came from and where you're going.

I can always navigate ✦ ✦ my way back to calm.

WRITE IT OUT

Take stock of your proverbial backpack. Write down how you're feeling about the day ahead. Consider your metaphorical true north, and identify today's activities that align with your personal goals and dreams. If you look at the list and feel anxiety about the activities that feel off your intended path, choose a few of the breathing techniques already discussed and begin practicing them to regain control. You can't always avoid stress and anxiety—they're part of life—but you can find your way back to calm.

Feel the Focus

The ironic thing about anxiety is that you're actually great at focusing (yay!)—just on the wrong things (boo!). If you're like most people, you are probably an expert at focusing on all that might go wrong and maybe a little less practiced at focusing on all that could go well.

Negativity can be a downward spiral. You know the deal: Something makes you anxious or stressed, and before you know it, the least likely, worst-case scenario feels inevitable. You feel like you're headed toward disaster and can't escape it.

What would happen if you shifted your attention? What if you practiced refocusing your thoughts on something uplifting? What if you imagined things going well? When you do, you can bring positivity back into focus. Hope begets hope, and before you know it, your stress dissipates.

We want to be realistic here. Sometimes it isn't possible to escape stress entirely. Anyone who has ever had papers due, bills to pay, or little kids running around knows that life comes with built-in stressors that you can't ignore. But you do have control over your mindset, and shifting your thoughts toward positive outcomes can be transformative.

CHANGE YOUR FOCUS

Try the rule of twenty-twenty-twenty.[2] Take a break of twenty seconds every twenty minutes by looking at something twenty feet away. Often used to take breaks from a screen to prevent eyestrain, this is a helpful technique for those experiencing burnout at work and for those who need to shift their perspective to stop an anxiety spiral.

AFFIRMATION

I will shift my focus toward things that calm me.

DAY 7

Protect the Pause

Remember the last time you watched a sports game? (For some of you, that may have been a long time ago, but go with it.) In any game of soccer or basketball or football, you'll typically see players and coaches calling for a time-out periodically. You know why? Even the athletes at the top of their game need time to collect themselves, mentally and physically. The time they spend on themselves pays off.

Whether it's because you genuinely don't feel like you can ask your toxic boss for a breather or you feel guilty (or silly or weak) for needing a break from your kids, hear this: There is no shame in needing a break. Taking a day off or setting aside a few minutes to regroup could mean the difference between emotional upheaval and emotional control.

Pausing is key to stopping the stress spiral. It's important to build designated breaks into your calendar and then set a firm boundary around those breaks. Practicing and protecting your pauses, even when you don't feel like you need them, makes it easier to ask for them when you do.

I will pause when it is necessary to collect my calm.

CALL A TIME-OUT

Hit pause on your to-do list today. It doesn't matter how long it is. Set a timer for ten minutes and take an actual break. That means no screens, no interruptions. We're serious! No cheating, people! Taking this break (and making a regular practice of it) gives you the time to collect your thoughts and encourages you to hit pause—no matter what's stressing you out.

Calm the Storm

There's a reason emotions have been described as tempests. With the many (many) emotions that you feel swirling at any given moment, it's easy to get swept up. One minute you're innocently thinking about school pickup, that big presentation at work, or whether you have time to prepare your lunches for the week; the next, you're swept up in a storm of worry, fear, stress, and anxiety.

As the storm of negative emotions swirls within you, you might feel as if you can stand firm and strong. But sometimes the storm is a nasty one, and you feel yourself losing your grip on reality. Lightning strikes, thunder claps, the waves batter your ship. It can feel chaotic and scary, especially since you don't know when the storm will end.

Here's the thing about storms: They only exist under the right conditions. While you can't control the external pressures and high temperatures your life may bring, you *can* learn to take control of the conditions in your mind. When you do, you'll be able to see how life's storms can dissipate into a beautiful day.

SMOOTH SAILING

Imagine a ship in a storm. Then imagine yourself inside the bow of the ship, tucked into the sleeping quarters safe and sound. (Don't worry, someone very smart and capable is at the helm!) Now you can close your eyes. Imagine a warm heater at your feet, a cozy blanket wrapped snug around you. Look at the walls and imagine a series of paintings there. What do you see? Observe them and honor them. No wrong answers. Remember that as life throws you into stressful situations, you have the power to control your peace, one restful moment at a time.

— AFFIRMATION —

I have the ability to calm the storm of anxiety inside me.

Practice Release

Battling anxiety can feel like playing a nonstop game of tug-of-war. There are days when you're winning and feeling unstoppable, and there are others when you're barely hanging on as your spiraling thoughts yank you down. On those days, you lose your footing, your grip falters, and when you try to rally more energy, it's quickly wasted on the fight.

If you're locked in this mind game, remember *you're* the one holding the rope. You have a choice: Let your fears upset your balance and pull you over the line, *or* let go of the rope while you're still standing. Know that there is no shame in forfeiting this game today, if that's what is healthiest for you. Sometimes walking away in the middle of your tug-of-war game with anxiety is actually winning.

If fear is overwhelming you, it may be time to drop that rope and engage with a soothing activity. You are not quitting. There will be other times to take up the rope to address your anxiety. Know you can step away from the tug-of-war mind games until you feel better regulated. Open your hands and drop the rope.

I can release ✦ things that are out of ✦ my control.

LET IT GO

Let's add a physical movement to this act of letting go. Write down on small scraps of paper the things that are making you feel anxious. Crumple them up and choose one to clutch in your fist. Grip it firmly. Inhale, and when you exhale, release your grip, watching it fall to the floor. Repeat this practice until no paper remains. Observe the pile of worry littering your floor and reflect on how much lighter it feels to let go of the stress that was weighing on your mind. These thoughts and worries have no power over you.

DAY 10

Clear Out the Clutter

Ticket stubs and books you've forgotten to return to friends, greeting cards from high school graduation, expired beauty products, clothes that no longer fit . . . whether you're holding on to these things—knickknacks, trinkets, tchotchkes, whatever you call them—for sentimental value or because you haven't had the time to organize, the truth is this: Our lives are full of *things*.

Your brain is constantly looking for order and patterns (that's why it's so good at spotting patterns that set off your fight-or-flight response),[3] and if the space around you is cluttered, your brain is cluttered.[4] When all you can see around you is *disorder*, your brain will act accordingly. This is terrible news for messy people, we know. We're not telling you to throw out everything you own, but simply to ask yourself: *What do I really need? What actually makes me happy?*

Take stock of what's important to you and make a practice of letting go of things that no longer hold meaning to you. Spending time accepting that change is *good*, and that you can let go, is a great way to solidify what you've learned about releasing tension and anxious thoughts.

I will let go of what no longer serves me.

UNCLUTTER YOUR LIFE

Let's take this one small space at a time. Come on, just five minutes. Go to a messy shelf, a drawer, or a nook in your house that's been causing you stress. Look for duplicates, unused items, and things you haven't touched in the past year. Choose a box or bag designated for donations. Spend just five minutes each day and watch how that space transforms over time. We aren't advising that you suddenly become a minimalist if that's not your style, but when you unclutter your life, feel your brain respond in kind.

DAY 11

Explore Your Creativity

We can hear some of you now: "I'm not a creative person." We mean this in the politest way we can say it: *Pishposh*! You do not need to know how to paint, sing, draw, dance, or embroider to be considered creative. (Although if you do any of these things, please keep it up!)

You are creative every single day, whether you know it or not. You use your creativity to put together a presentation at work, to figure out how to entertain the kids while making dinner, or to pack a suitcase for an upcoming trip. Don't sell yourself short about your creative potential! It is special and specific to you.

Using your creativity is one way to alleviate anxiety and stress,[5] and chances are, there are opportunities to be creative all throughout your day! Your job is to identify when and how you can embrace your creative side and take advantage of it. When you are creative, your body relaxes, and you can focus on something other than your anxious thoughts or endless to-do list. You can reframe your tasks at work or chores around the house as creative endeavors.

EMBRACE YOUR INNER CHEF

We all gotta eat! Every meal you make at home is an opportunity to embrace your creativity. That delicious dish you've seen on TikTok and keep meaning to make but never do? Today is the day! Dash out to the store or order ingredients on your favorite app. Watch how the task of making dinner becomes a homemade adventure. Let the flavors and smells transport you into a state of calm and joy.

———— AFFIRMATION ————

I can embed creativity ✦ into my daily ✦ practices.

DAY 12

Look for the Positives

W hen calm feels far away, anxiety encourages you to focus on all the things that are going (and could go) wrong. Even if you're a generally positive person, anxiety and stress have a way of making it difficult to see the good around you. Then, every negative thing you see becomes a confirmation of why you actually *should* feel anxious. Confirmations feel good, in part because they make you feel like the time you spent worrying wasn't wasted.[6] But what would happen if, instead of looking for confirmations of the bad, you looked for evidence of the good?

Practicing positivity can feel difficult, even impossible at times. There will be moments when it feels like you don't deserve to be positive and others when it simply feels too hard. Start small, bestie. It can begin with the little, seemingly insignificant things that make you smile. When in doubt, latch on to these truths: You *deserve* to feel positive. You *deserve* to find calm. It all starts with looking.

I will conquer the day with a positive mindset.

ADD IT UP

Make a game of finding the positives today. Using your phone or a piece of paper, tally up your items of positivity and see how many "points" you accumulate throughout the day. Whenever you see something that makes you smile or think a positive thought, add a point to your record. Doing this will have you on the lookout for the positives when your anxiety wants you to point out the negative. Try to beat this number, day by day.

DAY 13

Find Joy in Movement

How do you feel about exercise? It's a tricky topic; so many of us have a complicated relationship with moving our bodies. What would happen if you thought of movement as a means to bring yourself joy or show yourself gratitude, rather than as a punishment, obligation, or means to an end?

Movement can be joyous! You've heard of the endorphins that flood your brain,[7] lowering stress and improving your mood. But also, with some exploration, you might find an activity you really love. And, hey, if you consider yourself to be a clumsy person and the only thing you can focus on during movement is not tripping and falling, at the very least, your thoughts are no longer on what is making you anxious. Finally, a "win" for those of us who had perpetually skinned knees as children.

If you have negative thoughts around exercise, this won't change overnight, and in the short run, this practice could feel counterintuitive to finding your calm. But if you start experimenting with movement bit by bit, you may just find a form that works for you.

GET MOVING

Choose a movement practice that you love. Give yourself permission to admit which movements serve you and which do not. It can be as regimented as a cycling class or as informal as a dance party to your favorite pump-up playlist. Gentle movements like a walk or yoga can do wonders for your mental health.[8] Connect to your body in a way that feels good and joyous. This not only releases those oh-so-nice endorphins,[9] but also releases any tension you're holding, bringing you joy in the process.

--- AFFIRMATION ---

I will ✦ connect with ✦ my body by moving it.

DAY 14

Let Go of Control

When you let anxiety and stress drive your day, you may find yourself trying to control everything and everyone. That's because, when you're feeling out of control in one area (whatever is making you feel anxious), it feels good to find *something* to have control over. But the reality is, for better or worse, you're never going to have *full* control over your life.

Here's the good news today: Some things *are* within your control. You are a person with agency, so let's dive in and assess what's in your control today. These things generally fall into three categories: your thoughts, your actions, and your reactions. Are you sensing a theme? *You* are the common denominator. You *can't* control other people's actions or reactions, or whether they do the right (or wrong) thing, or what they think. People gonna people, as we like to say.

When you focus on what you alone can control, you take responsibility for yourself without taking on the burden of others. You've got you! And we know you're fab! Focus on your own agency, and watch anxiety fall away.[10]

I cannot control others, but I can control myself.

IDENTIFY IT

At the top of a page in your journal, describe your primary problem that's causing stress. Then start a list of what you can control about the problem. Divide between tasks that you can implement immediately and some that take more time. Create a plan to chip away at that list, and trust you have what it takes to keep moving your life forward. Whenever you feel anxious thoughts creeping in, return to this list and focus on what you can control, rather than what you cannot.

DAY 15

Rest and Replenish

Any of this sound like you? You wake up tired, check your calendar, and feel a cascade of dread. Coffee. You tend to your pets and kids, jump into work, run errands during lunch. More coffee. You rush to school for pickup, dash home, fold a load of laundry. More coffee, maybe? You somehow manifest a dinner, send one last email, get to bed late, scroll through social media (even though you promise you'll give it up someday, but that day is not today). Finally, you fall asleep, wake up, and do it all over again.

Tired? Sleep is one of your greatest defenses against stress. Unfortunately, stress can cause a lack of sleep.[11] And when you don't get enough sleep, you're more prone to poor focus or brain fog, a weakened immune system, and weight gain.[12] Many of us rely on stimulants like coffee to get us through, but they're never enough.

It may feel like you have no control over how much sleep you get, but there are steps you can take to get better, more consistent rest, namely revamping your sleep routine and setting boundaries around your schedule.

REVAMP YOUR SLEEP ROUTINE

This week, take note of what time you go to bed, what you do when you get into bed, and how or when you feel most comfortable. What can you do to make your nighttime routine truly restful? Here are a few things we suggest: Put away electronics an hour before bed, take a warm bath, sip herbal tea, or practice meditation. Choose one, and count them sheep, bestie.

AFFIRMATION

Protecting my sleep gives me more ✦ ✦ energy for the journey.

DAY 16

Pause the Productivity

I t's easy for an outside observer to tell you to simply slow down when, in your reality, it feels anything but simple. After spending your time frenetically chasing productivity in your workplace, with your family, in your hobbies, and all the other areas in life, *un*productivity feels alien. Worse, the feeling of being unproductive can leave you feeling inadequate.

Newton's first law of motion states that an object in motion stays in motion, and an object at rest will stay at rest.[13] This can feel especially true in times of anxiety and uncertainty. You may feel like your only option is to keep on moving—or that if you rest for even one moment, you'll never get going again. But if you don't take a break, this is how burnout happens.

No matter what you have been told, you do not need to be *producing* to be *productive*. You are just as adequate at rest as you are at warp speed. You are productive in everything that you do, simply by being who you are and chasing your joy.

I am productive when I pause and do not need to rush.

MAKE A WON'T LIST

Take time today to make a list of things you will not be doing. (These are our favorite kinds of lists!) These can be things that don't serve you (byeeeee) or things you don't have time for. Let this list serve as a reminder that you are already productive enough without piling on to your productivity. Be just as proud of the things you did not accomplish today as the things you did.

Stand Tall

Ever notice that you're hunched over, cross-armed, cross-legged, and slumped down into yourself? (And did you just sit up a little straighter after reading that? We love to see that, friend!) The effects of stress and burnout don't just happen in your mind, they also happen to your body.

While poor posture can of course contribute to physical problems, it also substantially impacts the way you feel.[14] If you're not mindful about it, you might become so comfortable pulling inward that you stop looking around to notice new and exciting things. Before you know it, you lose confidence in yourself and the world around you. As your body folds in on itself, your world grows smaller, and your perspective does too.

In nature, we value and admire things that grow, stretch, or take up space. Think of a tree sinking its strong roots into the ground and reaching its branches toward the sky. Or a mountain you admire in the distance—immovable and unchanging from base to summit. Now think of yourself at your most confident, standing firm like a mountain or tree, taking up space and exuding strength.

BE THE MOUNTAIN

Mountain pose (or tadasana) is a yoga pose that can help you feel balanced, strong, and confident.[15] Stand with your feet hip-distance apart. Align your shoulders over your hips and your hips over your ankles. Arms should be at your side with your palms forward as you look straight ahead. Add confidence to your pose by lifting your chest and pulling your shoulders back and down. Take some time to breathe and set your intention for the day.

AFFIRMATION

I will stand tall and open my chest, exuding the confidence I want to embody.

BODY

DAY 18

True to Your Heart

O ne of the best things about a dog park is watching pups of all shapes, sizes, and ages become friends. That baby Pomeranian yapping at the wide-eyed greyhound? That Westie-Doberman bestie situation? *Be still our ever-loving hearts*. If you're a pup kind of person, observing all their different personalities and quirks can be an endless source of curiosity and joy. We love all of them for exactly who they are.

What if we learned to look at ourselves with the same kind of openness and curiosity? One of the things that robs us of our calm is the belief that we have to morph ourselves to be like someone else. That we must fit a certain "type" in order to succeed. When you absorb others' expectations for your life, it's easy to believe the narrative that you're failing when, actually, it's possible that these expectations are simply a bad fit for who you are and who you want to be. (Bestie, if you're a Chihuahua, be the Chihuahua!)

Today, we encourage you to consider: What are your strengths, and how much of your day is organized around what you're good at? Where do you need to adjust rhythms in your life to better align with who you are, instead of who someone else wants you to be?

38

CELEBRATE YOU

Hold a hand over your heart and take a few deep breaths. Feel your heart beneath your palm. As you inhale, name something you're good at. Like really good at. As you exhale, release one expectation placed upon your life that you intend not to meet. These may be difficult to name at first, but keep returning to this practice until you find clarity.

I honor my ✦ strengths and ✦ release others' expectations for my life.

DAY 19

Pencil *You* In

Y ou can tell a lot about someone's state of mind by looking at their calendar. It's a window into a person's inner life, a vulnerable space that shows what they value and care about most. A disorganized, stuffed-to-the-brim calendar is a surefire signal that you're probably headed toward chaos. But y'all, the good news is, this is fixable! Regulation is within your reach.

Maybe you're the kind of person who makes several plans while you are feeling great, but after a few weeks of going nonstop, you burn out. Or maybe you're the kind of person who says "yes" even when you know you shouldn't, simply because you don't want to disappoint your friends or colleagues. People-pleasing, overscheduling, and over-committing are responses to *and* causes of anxiety.[16] These behaviors leave little room for self-care and reflection.

Your calendar (physical or digital) should be sacred to you on this journey to find calm. If you care about finding your peace, then you need to make time to do so. If you're looking at the month ahead and noticing there is no space for you, chances are you'll have a hard time finding peace and calm there too—unless the plans are for an all-inclusive vacation lying on a beach, then we take that back.

I can keep my sights on a calm horizon.

PENCIL IN YOUR PEACE

Open your calendar. If that sentence made you cringe, be kind to yourself. Look at the month ahead. There will be commitments you can't avoid, important events you've already RSVP'd to, dates already blocked. Look ahead to the empty spaces. Are there any you can claim? Go ahead, pencil yourself in. Block it off and treat it as if you promised the time to someone else.

DAY 20

Feel It Out

We've been talking about stress and anxiety in broad terms, but it's time to dig into specifics. When you get specific about your feelings around stress, you may find that you're actually feeling overwhelmed, out of control, or rushed. When you're feeling anxious, you might dig deeper to find feelings of helplessness, fear, or inadequacy. When you pull back the curtain, burnout may be a symptom of exhaustion, depression, frustration, or numbness. And these are just a few examples.

You are a complex individual who can feel multiple things at one time. When you're in the middle of an anxious or stressful season, it can seem easier to push your feelings down, minimizing them rather than admitting them. "I'm just a little stressed" becomes a pat excuse for the ocean of unmet emotional and physical needs you're avoiding.

Give it a try. What would happen if you acknowledged that you're scared, or worried, or disappointed, or whatever emotional cocktail you might've concocted? When you name your feelings, you can address them more specifically and ask for help more easily. When you know what it is you need, you can address it and move toward a more calm and peaceful self.

GET IN YOUR FEELS

Grab a pen and paper and write down five things you see around you. (Good job! It's not a blank page anymore! You've started writing, and we think that's the hardest part.) Now, take a look around your emotional landscape and get specific about what you're feeling without judgment. Write as fast as you can for thirty seconds. Stand up and jump ten times (motion moves emotion[17]); now get back in that chair. Pick one emotion on your list and take sixty seconds to make a word cloud around this singular feeling. Come back to this list tomorrow to nonjudgmentally observe the words that poured out of you. Getting specific will help you root out what's at the heart of your anxiety so you can address it.

--- AFFIRMATION ---

I can identify my emotions to understand what I need.

DAY 21

Working Outside In

H ave you ever been in a situation when you felt a complete sense of calm and confidence, even if you weren't sure where it was coming from? Maybe it was a time when you were sticking up for a good friend or giving a presentation at work. How would you describe your body language in these calm moments?

For most of us, we may describe a sense of rootedness. Calm is associated with feeling grounded, two feet firmly planted to the floor. In these moments, we feel supported by the physical foundation beneath us, empowering us to physically stand tall and not slouch. We take up more space because we trust the earth to hold us.

Our physical bodies are wonderful cues to our emotions. But it doesn't stop there! We can actually shift our emotional states by adjusting our physical ones. If you're stuck in a cycle of mind games and can't seem to clear your head, that's okay. Maybe the mental tactics you're trying won't work today! That's why we have more tools in our tool kit to reclaim our calm. Today, let's focus on making physical shifts and trust that the mental and emotional ones will follow.

I can rely on my body to tell me when I'm stressed.

FIND YOUR WEIGHT

Your body knows when you're overwhelmed, and if you want to connect back to yourself, you must honor its knowledge. How? Sit still and listen. You can do this anywhere. Find a comfortable position and take a few deep breaths. Focus on any limb or muscle group and pay attention to the weight on the underside portion of that body part, wherever it rests on the ground or the piece of furniture you're sitting on. Let this heaviness seep in and take joy in it. Stay here and keep breathing, until you sense yourself starting to release. If your body feels incredibly tense, it's a good cue you may need to plan for some intentional time off.

DAY 22

Be Kind to Yourself

Has anyone told you lately how wonderful you are? Sure, it's easy to believe that about other people who seem to race through life with abandon. Somehow, they just *have* it. It can make you feel like *you* aren't as capable, which can lead to negative self-talk.

Friend, we're not doing that anymore. Negative self-talk can include belittling yourself and your experiences, blaming yourself unfairly, being overly critical, or assuming the worst in a situation. It can make you question your worth, which is one thing that should never be questioned. Say it along with us: *I am worthy of peace and happiness.* Say this again and again until it feels authentic to you.

To battle negative self-talk, practice doing the opposite and speak positively about yourself. This might feel really difficult at times. That's why it's important to make it a regular habit, so it feels more natural to you.

Talking kindly to yourself can improve not only your mood in the short term, but also your self-esteem in the long term. This in turn can have a huge impact on how you react to situations, people, places, and circumstances that cause you stress and anxiety.[18] Sounds like a much better way to go through life, don't you think?

I deserve to treat myself with kindness.

COMPLIMENT YOURSELF

The anxious voice in your head isn't always a truth-teller. You have inherent worth. You are incredible. And you deserve to treat yourself with kindness. Look at yourself in the mirror and combat those negative thoughts by giving yourself a compliment. It's that simple. Tell yourself the truth about who you are and what you love about yourself. When you make a regular practice of speaking kindly to yourself, it's easier to grab hold of truth when peace feels far away.

Finish Strong

No matter how many calming activities you do, no matter how often you gain control of your emotions, there's always a chance that you will simply have a bad day. It's inevitable, in fact, because although you may have control over yourself and your thoughts, you don't have control over the actions of others. And let's be honest: Some of those *others* can get on your last nerve.

It's tempting to dwell on the emotions of your day, even after it's over. How you spend your day, no matter how you feel about it, does not need to be an indicator of how you'll end it. A bad day doesn't have to turn into a bad night.

Rather than letting those emotions and feelings carry over into the evening, spend some time processing them. Journal or talk it out with a trusted friend. It may be helpful to set a timer for yourself so you don't dwell on it for too long. (We've all been there.) Then do something that makes you feel good so you can reset and finish strong.

END ON A HIGH

Tonight, do something you enjoy before bed. Watch a favorite show, enjoy a bowl of ice cream, try some yoga flows, or pull out a coloring book. Whatever you do, remember that you can end your day differently from how it started. Give yourself a sense of accomplishment by finishing with your own personal joy.

— AFFIRMATION —

I am in control of how I close my day.

Check, Please!

Have you ever had one of those days when you're so busy that you look up at the clock and realize it's already dinnertime? *Where did the day go?* This feels like a yellow flag to us. If you consistently lose track of time and are living your life in a rushed state, let's check in to ensure you're feeling mentally healthy.

There is only one rule to checking in on yourself: Be honest. So first, let's look at some phrases that could be signs you're being *dishonest* with yourself. Thoughts like, *I'm fine, I'm just being dramatic* or *It's not that bad, I can handle it* or *I'll just figure it out, it's okay* are signs that you might be minimizing your feelings and putting too much pressure on yourself.

Instead, challenge yourself to ask, *How am I doing? No, really. How am I doing?* Describe your emotions; don't rush past them. If your boss is pressuring you with unrealistic deadlines, you can remind yourself, *That behavior is actually not okay, and I'm upset by it.* Slowing down, naming your emotions, and checking in to see how you *really* feel about a situation begets more trust in yourself. You can rely on your own intuition, and you can move at your own pace.

CHECK YOUR SPEED

It's time to treat yourself as you would your best friend. A good friend is concerned with your well-being and is quick to ask how you are. Grab a journal to reflect on how you're really doing. Write about why you feel pressured to move so fast. Identify who or what is causing you to feel that time squeeze, and release your need to people please. This is your one life—no one else's—and you can move at the pace that's healthy for you.

I can be a best friend to myself and check in to see what I need.

DAY 25

Get Your Groove Back

We all know you can't laugh and panic at the same time. So if something is nagging at your thoughts or causing you to grind your teeth, let's break the cycle and invite in some humor. Call that friend who makes you laugh. Step away from the computer and turn on your favorite comedy special. Let laughter overtake you, and give yourself permission to enjoy your life. The hard stuff will wait. Today, we play!

What would it look like to embrace a spirit of spontaneity? There's something particularly freeing about getting a little bit goofy, doing something unexpected, trying something new, and letting loose once in a while. Joy is a muscle, and you have to work it if you want to strengthen it!

If you find yourself missing a sillier version of yourself, this is your reminder that this version of you still exists. And we think that version of you is so much fun! With all you have going on, that part of you might not be as easy to access these days, but practice makes progress, as they say. Relax, do something for yourself, and leave your anxious thoughts behind for a moment.

I am getting ✦ my groove back, one day at a time. ✦

DANCE IT OUT

Need a suggestion for something silly? We have so many, but for today, try dancing. Don't worry about whether you're a "good" dancer. In fact, we'd argue that rhythm is not required at all. Just turn on your favorite tunes, close the door, and get back into the groove. Extra points if you also sing at the top of your lungs.

MIND

DAY 26

Set Your Routine

S tress doesn't seem to obey the rules of time. When you're stressed, some minutes feel like hours, and some hours feel like minutes. This sensation can leave you feeling disoriented and dysregulated. You're hyperproductive one day and crashing the next. What's an overachieving person like you to do? We got you.

As simple as it sounds, a wonderful way to reduce stress is by creating a regular routine for yourself—and here's the catch: Stick to it. Creating a routine can help reduce anxiety[19] because you're following a plan that you *know* already works, taking the guesswork out of your day where you can. And this way, you can even plan in some cushion for things to go wrong (because, let's be real, they will).

After you've stuck to your routine for a little while, you'll likely find that your sleep schedule becomes more regular, that it's a little less daunting to get to the gym, and a little easier to prep and cook your meals. After all, you've already scheduled these activities into your day. Though scheduling your day may feel restricting, you're actually giving yourself a ton of freedom—freedom to prioritize what's important, and a structure to rely on when things are difficult.

MAKE PEACE PART OF YOUR ROUTINE

Open your calendar for the next month and gather your to-do list. First, book personal time for yourself each day. Then place every task from your to-do list onto your calendar. Allocate the amount of time you think that task will take—do not cheat yourself! Highlight your main priorities. (And no, not everything is a priority!) If you notice you're overbooked, look at the non-highlighted tasks. Reach out to your respective colleagues, spouse, family members, or friends who may be counting on you, and give them advance notice you won't be hitting your deadline. They may be disappointed, but that's okay. Your peace is yours to protect.

—————— AFFIRMATION ——————

✦ I will prioritize what is ✦ important.

DAY 27

Be a Problem Solver

Have you ever put a jigsaw puzzle together? The picture on the front of the box doesn't just manifest itself; you have to put some time in. You clear space on the table and turn all the pieces face up so you can see what you're doing. Then you separate the edges from the middle pieces and start working on the border. You then begin putting together the center, using the picture as a guide and working in sections to complete the picture.

When you feel out of control, imagine that the problems you're facing are just one big jigsaw puzzle. Take it one piece at a time. Flip the facts over so you can see them all straight. Then, metaphorically, assemble the frame. To do this, repeat your core values and priorities to yourself, as these are the frame of your life. Once you center yourself in what matters most and find a sliver of calm to connect to, then you can grab your calendar and begin to consider the solutions, moving one piece—or one step—at a time.

Puzzles can be put together in many ways, of course, so stay open to the idea that there could be multiple ways to solve your problems. You've solved puzzles and worked through problems before, and you can do this one too. Take your time and be proud of the finished product.

I can tackle my problems methodically without spiraling.

PUZZLE IT OUT

Did you know that doing puzzles can have several mental health benefits, including stress reduction?[20] Find a puzzle today. It can be a jigsaw puzzle, sudoku, or a crossword puzzle online or in the newspaper. Take your time completing it and accept when you make a mistake or can't figure out an answer on your own. If it's a crossword, call or text a friend when you need a hint. Heck, even use the internet if you're getting desperate. Sometimes you just need reminding that you are capable of solving a puzzle, even if it requires some help along the way.

DAY 28

Keep Going and Embrace the Mud

Before you head out on a hike, there's often a map that marks the difficulty of each trail, offering a two-dimensional look at a very three-dimensional terrain. The map depicts which terrain will be easiest and which will be hardest. But unless you've hiked there recently, you won't know what kind of terrain you'll be met with. Stone, dirt, mud—why don't they list *that* on a map? (National parks, we're looking at you.) Still, you came to hike, so you set out.

Each day, you set out with an idea of what's to come. What you find, however, may surprise you. Could be a waterfall, could be mud swirling with gnats. But the most resilient people in this world have a way of seeing beauty in the dirt, finding potential in untended soil. There is beauty to be found in the journey, joy to be found in the struggle. Embrace a spirit of openness and curiosity, and keep your eyes peeled for something wonderful.

And maybe today comes and goes—and it goes really bad. Like a hailstorm kind of bad. But you know what? You came to hike, and you're going to see yourself through to the end. You're always so good at that!

There is beauty in the journey.

TAKE A HIKE

Even if you're not outdoorsy, and even if you can't go today, research hiking paths near you that match your skills and ability and plan for a hike. It doesn't need to be difficult or lengthy—just enough for you to spend time on a trail, taking in the nature around you and enjoying the journey. Turn your phone off please (okay, fine, except for your maps app . . . we get it). As you go, take note of what you see and hear along the way. If it starts to rain? Even better. You can experience beauty even in less-than-perfect conditions with the proper attire.

DAY 29

Get Real About It

Expectations are assumptions that you make about the future based on experiences you've had in the past or things you've observed. You might have expectations about a trip you're going on after seeing an influencer hype it up on social media. Or maybe you have expectations that your boyfriend will propose to you a certain way because that's what you've seen in rom-coms. You might expect to perform poorly on a test or during a presentation because, after all, that's what happened last time.

Expectations aren't inherently bad. They can be helpful in keeping you safe. But it's important that you take the time to understand your expectations and create realistic ones to avoid the undesirable emotional lows that come with them being unmet or missed.

You have the power to monitor your thoughts and focus on creating expectations that are realistic while still remaining hopeful and optimistic. Give yourself permission today to ask questions about your expectations for your life. Where did they come from? Are your expectations for yourself rooted in reality? Are you expecting yourself or others in your life to be perfect? How can you better advocate for yourself to normalize your own humanity?

CHECK YOUR EXPECTATIONS

We often stress because we expect things to go wrong, and then we expect it to be a huge deal when they do. Think about an event or task up ahead that's causing you stress. Let's take time to set the scene realistically. Before charging ahead toward whatever you're anxious about, imagine that nothing goes wrong. In fact, imagine it goes great! Then imagine that something does go wrong, but this time, see yourself handling this mishap with grace and dignity. Because one thing we know about you? You're capable! Set realistic expectations so you don't stress unnecessarily.

───── **AFFIRMATION** ─────

I can set reasonable expectations for myself and others.

Stop and Smile

O*of*, nothing is worse than someone telling you to smile when you don't feel like it. Well, hear us out, because while we don't think it's helpful in *all* circumstances, finding something to smile about *is* a useful tool to battle a spiral of stress or anxiety. But this time, it's on *your* terms.

Before we go further, this is *not* a call for you to bypass your emotions. You shouldn't put on a happy face and pretend everything is okay if it isn't, and you don't need to smile to make other people feel comfortable. Express yourself truthfully and ask for help if needed.

We *are*, however, encouraging you to take the time to seek things in your life (past, present, and future) that spark joy and bring you happiness and reminding you that stress and anxiety are temporary. When you're feeling stressed or anxious, you can hit pause, think of a happy memory or picture something you love, and begin to feel joy again, pulling yourself out of your spiral.[21] It doesn't mean your anxiety disappears forever, but that momentary break gives your brain something else to focus on and hits pause on the pattern.

I can smile even in the face of stress.

CREATE A SMILE FILE

A "smile file" is a break-in-case-of-emergencies compilation of things that make you happy. This can include your favorite videos or memes on the internet, movies from your childhood, photos you took on your last trip with friends, poems, songs, quotes, or stories that never fail to make you smile or laugh. This smile file is a spot you can return to often to give yourself a boost. Be sure to add to it as you find new things to smile about.

SPIRIT

It's the Small Stuff

Because we're often told not to sweat it, the "small stuff" gets a bad rap when, in fact, the small stuff can be a source of immense calm and joy. Focusing on the little things that make the world beautiful can be a fantastic practice in cultivating presence, perspective, and inner peace.[22]

The laugh of a child reminds you there's joy to be found in the simplest of games. The rustle of leaves reminds you that change is always in the air. Stress and anxiety might make the world seem ugly or inconvenient, but simply changing your focus can remind you the world is amazing. When you are consumed by anxiety, you could be tempted to ignore the small but *good* things in life, and a key part of finding calm is recalibrating your focus to see the small beauties all around you.[23]

How lucky you are—no matter what's on your mind or how overwhelmed you are, you have a part to play in the world every single day. Meet that responsibility with gratitude and pay your respects to the little things around you.

✦ I will look for ✦ beauty all around me.

NOTE THE THINGS THAT SEEM SMALL

Sit outside today (phone off!) and look around. No, like, really look. Observe the trees growing, their roots strong in the ground, birds singing and soaring gracefully, flowers blooming. Maybe write down your favorites to return to later today when you feel overwhelm sneaking in. Even in your most anxious moments, you can rest assured that there is beauty in the growth you are experiencing. Practice this regularly, especially on days when you feel overwhelmed by how big everything feels.

Get Caught Trying

When you're young, it's natural to be a professional trier. Anyone who has seen or taken part in a middle school talent show knows this to be true. There was a time in life when you didn't think twice about signing up to dance with friends in front of the school. A time when you didn't minimize your accomplishments with an "it wasn't a big deal" or shy away from answering a question in class.

At some point, as you got older, you decided (whether consciously or unconsciously) that it was no longer cool or safe to get caught trying too hard. You recognized that to be seen trying is one of the most vulnerable things you can do because to try is to admit that you have the potential to fail. Maybe *trying* felt like *desperation* to you when it's actually an act of bravery. When failure and embarrassment are on the line, it's easy to get good at *not* trying.

What would your life look like if you gave yourself permission to try without worrying about the outcome? There is freedom in this mindset, and you may find yourself moving through your life with a lot more ease.

MAKE A TO-TRY LIST

Spend time today writing down anything and everything you'd like to try in the next few months. The time constraint allows you to be realistic, but if you'd like to dream big, go ahead! Think about the places you haven't been to in your area—maybe there's a new restaurant you've been meaning to check out or a cooking class you've been eyeing. Write them all down and make a plan for checking them off.

—— **AFFIRMATION** ——

I will find beauty in my determination to keep trying.

DAY 33

Move Through It

Though we often hear of two options in stressful situations—fight or flight—there is another response: to simply freeze.

Have you ever seen a play and watched an actor forget their lines? Many times, the actor becomes stiff and wordless, searching through the library of their mind for what happens next. Panic makes it even more difficult for them to find what they're looking for. If you've ever watched this happen live, it can feel absolutely miserable, even if you're not up on stage with them.

Common advice for actors in this predicament is to physically move and make a change in their bodies. Rather than standing rooted to the same spot, movement helps to deactivate that fight, flight, or freeze response that happens in stressful situations.[24]

When you find yourself going blank, give yourself some grace. You don't need to find the "next line" right away. Make a small change and move, reminding your body that the danger has passed.

I move gracefully through stressful situations.

NAME AND CHANGE

Remind yourself that you're in charge. Today, when you feel yourself becoming anxious, name your feelings and then make a change. The change doesn't need to be profound. Simply identify the feeling and change something— literally anything! It can be as small as sitting a different way or taking a short walk. Put both feet on the floor. Maybe pet a dog if you have one. Grab an old stuffed animal or trinket that brings you joy. Making these little changes reminds you that you have free will and power— two tools necessary to stop the spiral.

DAY 34

Be on the Lookout

Have you ever experienced the tunnel vision that often accompanies anxiety and stress?[25] Your imagination narrows in on the worst-case scenario, replaying fake scenes over and over in your mind. You become obsessed with all that could go wrong, leaning on the flimsy evidence around you that confirms your anxiety and ignoring what could alleviate it.

You're not doing this on purpose, and it's nothing to be ashamed of. But it is in these moments that stress and anxiety thrive. Because your brain can seem to focus only on what can go wrong, convincing you that the outcome cannot be changed, you lose sight of the many other possibilities that could go *well*.

Next time you find yourself experiencing tunnel vision from replaying the worst-case scenario, honor your imagination for preparing you for this scenario. Thank your anxiety for trying to protect you. And then, gently, challenge yourself to imagine the same situation with the exact opposite (best-case scenario) outcome. It may feel cringey at first, but practicing positivity becomes easier each time you try.

LOOK FOR IT

Next time you find yourself imagining a situation that hasn't happened yet, pretend you're a cinematographer and you're in control of that anxiety camera. (This is your imagination, after all!) Zoom all the way out and take note of something good and grounding in the foreground. Imagine yourself—get this—actually winning the conflict. Challenge yourself to identify the positives in the rooms of your imagination. The good is there; you just need the courage to let it in.

I am in control of the stories in my own imagination.

DAY 35

No More Shoulds

*S*hould is a loaded word. It indicates what we ought to do or ought to have done. It suggests there is only one right way to do anything. It's a common word for overthinkers and often leads to anxiety. It bombards us with thoughts like *I should have done that differently* or *I shouldn't complain* or *I should be less stressed*.

When you're constantly thinking about what you should have done or should be doing, get curious with yourself. Are you doing your best? Given the set of information you had at the time, would you do the same thing again? Are your standards realistic for yourself? Who are you trying to impress?

The reality is this: In most areas of life, there are multiple ways to get the job done. Parenting, advancing in your career, doing well at school, being a good friend. There's no singular "right" way to do any of this! When you make a decision, you are making the best one that you can with the information you have. In order to experience peace and calm in your life, eliminate *should* from your self-talk. Instead, give yourself some credit for being decisive and brave enough to accept the outcome.

I am doing my best, ✦ and I deserve ✦ compassion.

START A SHOULD JAR

Ever heard of a swear jar? Swap that out for a should jar. For every shaming should thought that enters your mind, go and stuff some cash in that jar. Hold yourself accountable, and measure how much money you've accumulated by the end of the month. Then take that money and spend it on yourself—just a small treat—and let this treat be a token of self-compassion and reclamation of the idea that you are doing your best with the information you have.

DAY 36

Don't Snooze! Choose You!

When you've had a particularly stressful day, you may go to bed believing that it'll all look better in the morning with fresh eyes. And you know what? Sometimes this is true. After all, adequate sleep can improve your stress levels, and sometimes a little distance can improve your perspective and frame of mind.[26] But other times, it's incredibly disappointing to find that you've woken up feeling just as overwhelmed as you did when you closed your eyes.

Don't let this discourage you. Your anxiety may not have disappeared overnight, but you can start your morning with a clear head.

You can make mornings meaningful and magical. (Somewhere, one of you night owls just rolled your eyes, but hear us out.) If you're the kind of person who hits snooze on your alarm, let us encourage you to replace that ten-minute snooze with an intentional morning pause. Any small moment to meditate, practice gratitude, or write out your thoughts can make all the difference in starting your day with a sense of peace rather than chaos.[27]

FILL UNFILTERED PAGES

In the morning, set a timer for ten minutes and just start writing. Write everything you're thinking, stream-of-consciousness style, without fear of judgment (from yourself or others). Describe what your day will look like, what you dreamed about, what you're anticipating, and how you're feeling. No wrong answers! Dumping all this information out of your brain and putting it all onto paper can offer perspective and help you feel calmer before starting your day.

I can start my morning with a clear head.

What's the Rush?

S top and smell the roses." A common refrain, but when you're overbooked and overwhelmed, it's the absolute last thing you want to be told.

Excuse me . . . stopping and smelling the roses would take up my precious, precious time, and I'm already behind. I'm late for my next meeting, barely had time for lunch, and I haven't called my best friend in a month. The roses, actually, respectfully, can wait their turn.

Anxiety and stress can make your time feel impossible to manage, like you can't stop for anything, let alone leisure. There is no shame in that feeling, but there is also no shame in hacking the system and *scheduling* time to stop and smell the roses, so to speak. Relying on a schedule or routine can help your brain transition from activity to activity in an orderly and organized way,[28] until you feel comfortable doing so spontaneously. It also helps you be honest about how much time you truly have in a day.

You deserve the break. Now make time to take it. Unfortunately, no one else is going to do this for you.

There is no rush. I can take my time.

PUT YOURSELF FIRST

For every day this week, challenge yourself to carve out time for you. Maybe you're in a very busy life stage and you have only fifteen minutes to spare. You know what? We'll take it. Set little dreams for yourself of how you will use this time—brewing your cup of coffee, reading before bed, or calling your bestie. These small moments of slowing down are a recognition of your humanity and help connect you back to yourself. You come first. (We mean it!)

DAY 38

Give Thanks

I f you woke up this morning burdened by heavy problems, there's a chance you rolled your eyes at the title of today's entry. It's difficult to hold on to gratitude when your arms are full.

But we all intrinsically know that gratitude is a gift in itself. The things you're grateful for right now may not feel profound. A phone call with a long-distance bestie, your favorite band's new single, silk sheets, a compliment about your outfit, a supportive word at work, the fact that rent didn't go up today. Seemingly small, daily activities—but so incredibly powerful in shifting the narrative you tell yourself about your life.

Starting and ending your day by practicing gratitude can change not only your attitude in the moment but your entire perspective. It gives you a taste of positivity when everything feels negative. It gives you hope and allows you to eventually share that hope with others. Gratitude is that secret superpower that interrupts all sorrow and stress and gives you the breath you need to press through the hard times.

PRACTICE THANKFULNESS

Start a gratitude practice this week. Spend five minutes in the morning, evening, or whenever you can fit space into your routine. Write down three things you are thankful for each day. They can be big, like a promotion at work or a day spent with family, or small, like the outfit you're wearing or the soft, clean sheets you sleep in. See how much you already have to be thankful for.

— AFFIRMATION —

I will practice gratitude every day.

SPIRIT

DAY 39

Locate Your Happy Place

You've seen it in movies: The main character is angry, anxious, or stressed. Enter: The best friend who puts their hands on their shoulders, looks them in the eyes, and says, "Go to your happy place." Cue: A dreamy montage of the main character's favorite place. When they return to the present, they're breathing easy and feeling calm.

There's a reason "finding your happy place" is a classic calming technique:[29] It works. It's not because you're dissociating from your real life; it's because you're taking your mind off what is making you anxious and focusing on positive things you can sense. Your happy place gives you a specific place to focus on that evokes fond memories.

If we asked everyone reading this book right now to describe their happy place, we bet no two would say the same thing. That's what makes it special—it's personal to you. You can do this while sitting in a stressful meeting at work, getting ready for a first date, or heading to a parent-teacher conference. There's no airfare or traffic to stop you. Be the jet-setter you've always longed to be, and give your happy place a visit today!

FIND YOUR HAPPY

Close your eyes and think of a place where you feel safe and peaceful. A beach you visited throughout childhood, the local deli, your dad's boat, your family's living room. Conjure up what it looks like, sounds like, smells like, and feels like. Imagine traveling to that destination, the excitement and contentment you experience. Drop in and imagine the breeze on your skin or the sun on your face or the comfy chair in the room. Visualize your happy place and practice taking a little mental vacation.

I can find calm in my happy place.

DAY 40

Get Unplugged

I t's tempting to open your phone within moments of waking up to check your texts and social media. In the modern era, there's a persistent feeling of *needing* to know what is always happening. You're not alone in feeling this way.

Just remember: Most things can wait. (Not all, but most.) It's going to be okay if you cocoon for a little while where no one can reach you. Experiment with this by keeping your phone off for an hour after waking up. Give yourself the gift of waking up with a peaceful, clear mind, rather than bombarding yourself with information right away.

It's just as tempting to sit in bed and scroll before you go to sleep. You tell yourself this time spent scrolling is relaxing or that you're just catching up from the day, but is it really? Not only does the light from your screen mess with your circadian rhythm,[30] but you're once again bombarding your brain with information when you're meant to be relaxing.

Protect these first and last moments of the day and see how it contributes to your calm.

I can take control of ✦ ✦ the start and end of my day.

START AND END SCREEN-FREE

Start and end your day without any screens. Ideally, give yourself an hour of screen-free time when you wake up and another hour before bed, but if you need to work up to that, there's no shame. If your phone alarm makes things too tempting, invest in an old-school alarm clock. If you can't trust yourself not to scroll (been there), many phones have screen time settings you can adjust to put time limits on certain apps.

DAY 41

Show Yourself Kindness

N o matter how old you are, you're doing *today* for the very first time. This is the first time you've lived through this exact set of circumstances. Think of children: When they are working something out for the first time, we view it as miraculous. We celebrate first steps and first words, even when they fall or pronounce something incorrectly. You can show yourself that same kindness. Self-compassion isn't selfish or self-pitying. It is an act of self-respect to honor the fact that you're not perfect.

Friends, try as we might, we're gonna mess up sometimes. You aren't perfect, and that means you're human!

Building a practice of self-compassion is key to combating stress.[31] Practicing being kind to and empathetic toward yourself often better equips you to self-soothe and replace your negative thoughts with positive ones. Self-compassion actually allows you to rebound more quickly, to become more resilient when things go wrong. It allows you to address mistakes with objectivity and improve yourself in the long run. When you employ this type of kindness in your thought life, you may even sleep better. So, friend, embrace a new day, celebrating your place in this world. Stay open to how you may grow within it. We're cheering for you.

WRITE YOURSELF A LETTER

To practice showing yourself compassion and kindness, write yourself a letter. Whatever you are anxious or stressed about, address it here, expressing your emotions without judgment. Then offer yourself some kindness. This can look like reminding yourself nobody is perfect, or forgiving yourself for your actions or reactions. When you take the time to show yourself compassion, you can accept that you are a beautiful work in progress.

I will champion compassion and kindness in my self-talk.

Clear the Smoke

Have you ever had a finicky smoke detector? The second something begins to brown, it beeps unrelentingly. You turn on the exhaust fan over the stove, wave a dish towel, open a window, but it's no match for that superhero smoke detector. (You just hope the upstairs neighbor isn't home to hear this . . . again.) Eventually you stop using the stove altogether and order takeout the rest of your life. (Kidding. Kind of.)

Anxiety is a lot like that smoke detector. It's there for a really good reason: to keep you safe. But if that alarm keeps going off, you either stop listening to it *or* you listen to it far too often and let it rule your life. In extreme cases, you stop doing the things altogether that set it off.

It might be time to calibrate your own alarm. You do this by noting what your triggers are and taking stock of how your body reacts to them. When you know what's making you anxious, you can then check in with your body, connect with your breath, and remind yourself that some things are not four-alarm fires—they're just burnt toast. (Scrape it off, grab some jam, and breakfast is served, my friend.)

I can use my breath to recalibrate myself.

TAKE A BREATH

Close your eyes and breathe in, counting to four and filling your lungs with air. Then, hold that breath for seven counts. Let out your breath, emptying your lungs of air, this time counting to eight. Repeat the cycle for up to four rounds. This 4–7–8 breathing technique can help alleviate stress and potentially reduce blood pressure, reduce the frequency and severity of migraines, and lead to an overall improvement in quality of life.[32] So take a 4–7–8 breathing break and try it for yourself!

Refuse the Rush

O pen your phone's voice memo app or grab a journal and describe your day yesterday. Go ahead, we'll wait.

Now look at the verbs used to describe your day. Look for words like *rushed*, *hurried*, *dashed*, *sped*, *raced*. As you consider what it means to find your calm in this new era of you, you must look at the literal speed at which you're moving through the world. If you're the kind of person who prides themselves on their speed, we know this might feel obnoxious. But . . .

There is beauty to be found when you choose to take things slow. This is not to say there won't be times when you'll be rushing or that others won't make you feel like you *have* to rush. It's inevitable that you'll wake up late one day or forget about dinner plans. But when it's in your control, you have the power to refuse the rush. When the world isn't passing by so quickly, it becomes easier to enjoy.

GO IN SLOW MOTION

Choose any part of your routine (one that doesn't have a deadline) and dare yourself to take double the time you would usually take to do it. Examples include taking thirty minutes for breakfast instead of your regular fifteen or taking a twenty-minute shower instead of ten. Whatever you choose to do, the idea is to simply take your time. Go in slow motion. Take time to notice and breathe. How do you feel? If it was difficult for you, practice makes progress!

AFFIRMATION

I will take pride in slowing down.

Have Good Intentions

Y ou've probably heard the opinion that intentions, even the best of them, mean nothing if they aren't accompanied with action. This is true of some situations, but when it comes to approaching your anxiety and stress specifically, what if setting good intentions is enough?

Hear us out. This is not permission to be passive, but rather an invitation to be kind to yourself. This journey to a calmer self will not be linear. You are allowed to try your best, fail, and accept your progress as it comes.

Here is your goal: Follow those good intentions over time. Your list of intentions is not a to-do list to be obsessively checked off. It is a road map that allows you to approach your day with positivity, and it has the power to change your interactions and experiences. Your progress may not be as immediate as you hope (this is part of what it means to be human), but you can confidently tell yourself that you did your best. Just keep heading in the right direction. Eventually, you will find your calm.

I have good ✦ intentions, and I will ✦ follow them.

SET YOUR INTENTIONS

We're halfway through this book, so let's start looking with a slightly longer view. Begin the day ahead by setting your intentions for the next year or so. You can create a list of things you intend to accomplish, and then dig deeper and think about what kind of attitude you would like to have while you accomplish them. Next to the list, write an emotion you'd like to feel after you're done. Be kind to yourself while setting these intentions and make them realistic. Keep this list in a spot that's visible and remind yourself of how you want to feel long term.

SPIRIT

Organizing Your Emotions

L et's start today by celebrating the fact that we have the capacity to feel a range of emotions. Part of what makes the human experience so rich is being able to experience the heights of happiness, compassion, and connection and, yes, even the lows of sadness, longing, and heartbreak. All feelings have a place in our lives.

Emotions aren't inherently bad, and if anyone has made you feel bad for having an emotion come up, we have some . . . well . . . *strong feelings* about that! They all serve a purpose.

No matter where you are today with your emotions, even if you're experiencing anxiety, know that your emotions are good, but they don't control you. Instead, usher in a spirit of curiosity to sift through them and seek to understand them. Carving out time to do this self-reflection will allow you to be more proactive in your life. Take some time today to sort through and honor your emotions—whatever they may be—but resist letting them take over. Ground yourself in what you know to be true: your values, your purpose, and who you are becoming.

TAKE FIVE

Is something giving you anxiety? Turn on a timer for five minutes. Talk to yourself, journal, or think about that scenario for five minutes. Feel what you need to without judgment. At the end of your five minutes, repeat this phrase: This is how I feel, and if I choose, I can let it go. Putting a timer on your anxiety in this way stops the spiral and encourages you not to let it take over your day.

— AFFIRMATION —

I can give myself time to feel and then let it go.

DAY 46

Don't Get Hooked on Hyper

A frenetic kind of energy accompanies stress. If we're honest, this frenetic energy can sometimes feel empowering. It can fuel us toward productivity, and we come to rely on it to achieve our goals and dreams. Does that sound familiar to you?

The problem is, when we become reliant on stress and anxiety to fuel us, things can go bad—fast. We feel out of control with obsessive thoughts flitting in and out of our minds. We move too quickly, never giving any task the focus it deserves. We feel like we're on a hamster wheel and can't get off. That frenetic rush starts to feel overwhelming. Maybe we even start to blame ourselves for feeling so out of control.

If this is resonating, y'all, we get it. You are not alone in this! Many of us have linked our fear with our productivity, and we want to work toward unraveling that. You can still find success without being chained to anxiety. Reinforce your peace by taking time for yourself to slow down, unwind, and practice self-care; then come back to your task at hand and practice working from a place of calm.

I have the power to slow down when I choose.

SLOW YOUR ROLL

If you continue to move at the speed you've been moving, the question isn't whether you'll burn out, but when. The moment you notice that you're feeling this way—even if you haven't experienced the negative effects yet—take some time. 👏 Turn off your phone, stop scrolling social media, meditate, read a book—it's up to you what this looks like. Don't let yourself get hooked on hyper. Be proactive and feel the power that comes when you prioritize slowing down.

DAY 47

You Are Enough

We all have a little voice inside our heads that tells us we're not enough and that the only way to *become* enough is to overextend and overcommit or to people please and change ourselves for someone else. Have you been listening to that voice lately? It's time to stop. That voice is lying to you. You do not have to be more than you are already. Spending time questioning your self-worth and comparing yourself to others is not serving you. This robs you of your calm and self-confidence you so rightly deserve. This is your one life; don't sacrifice your serenity to some liar in your head.

So let's replace these thoughts with a new one: You are enough. It's that simple! You do not need to add on one more meeting, stay later to prove yourself, or agree to plans you don't have time for (or don't want to attend in the first place). You do not need to compare yourself to the people you see on social media, that one coworker who seems to get the most praise, or your friend-of-a-friend who is (supposedly) so much happier than you. Their path is not yours. Stay the course and shut off that lying voice in your head. She's not invited here anymore.

ENOUGH IS ENOUGH

Sit up tall with proper alignment or lie down flat and long on your back. Close your eyes, then take a few deep breaths. Fill your lungs with air and then let your breath out slowly. On your inhale, repeat to yourself: I am enough. On the exhale, repeat: I will not compare. Do this for as long as you like. Connect with your breath and let it anchor you in these truths. You are enough. There is no need to compare yourself to others.

—— **AFFIRMATION** ——

I am enough; I will not compare.

DAY 48

Take a Time-Out

Were you a kid who got put in time-out a lot? For those who were better behaved than us as kids, here's the breakdown: You act out or break a rule, and an adult makes you stand in a corner for a chunk of time. When you're a kid, this seems excessive. The worst. Nothing worse has ever happened to a person *ever*. But with a fully developed adult brain, we can see that it's a powerful tool for self-regulating during stress or overwhelm.[33]

There will be times when you think, *I wish I could take a break, but [insert excuse for why you can't possibly take a break]*. Breaks can feel self-indulgent when you're overwhelmed. It's helpful, then, to resort to the old tried-and-true: a time-out.

Putting yourself in a time-out is not a punishment; it's a promise. It's a break you *have* to take. You're the adult in charge and you're not budging. When you take your time-out, you get to remove yourself for a moment, turn on a timer, and practice self-regulation. (Except, as an adult, we also recommend bringing snacks!)

When I'm ✦ overwhelmed, ✦ I can take a time-out.

PUT YOURSELF IN TIME-OUT

Today, when you feel yourself getting stressed, turn on a timer and put yourself in a time-out. Bonus points if your time-out spot is in its own space for a change of scenery from what's stressing you. Use that time to breathe, check in with your body, and find your calm. (And also, eat a cookie.)

DAY 49

Put Down the Pen, People!

Imagine you are watching your favorite author write a story about you. Sounds fun, right? They're coming up with interesting plotlines, surrounding you with people who love you and whom you love in return, and giving your character cool opportunities and experiences. The catch, they tell you, is that no, you cannot look over their shoulder while they brainstorm, or edit the story once they're done. You must trust the process. Do you do it?

When you are feeling out of control and anxious, it can be tempting to grab the pen, make a bunch of edits, and try to become the author of your entire universe. It may feel more comfortable to be in charge, but really, you end up limiting yourself.

What would happen if you let go of the pen? Just for today? Embrace the fact that you have limited control over what comes next in your story. Make wise choices, but also learn to embrace the unknown. Life is unfolding in all of its unexpected, twisty-turny glory. When you let your anxiety grab the pen to play it safe or edit out an experience, you're potentially missing out on some pretty amazing things that you could not have possibly written if you tried.

FOLLOW YOUR IMPULSES

Spend one day without making any plans. When that day comes, we want you to put on your good shoes, go out the front door, and just see what happens. This is a chance to follow your impulses or try new things. If one whole day is too much, try half a day or even an hour. If you have kids, you can include them. After all, no one is more spontaneous than a child.

✦ I will not skip ahead to write the end of this story.

✦

Honesty Is the Way Forward

When you're feeling overwhelmed, the default can sometimes be to admit defeat, throw up your hands, and say, "I'm a mess. I'm never going to change, and things never go my way!" And this may feel counterintuitive, but you know what? We're going to support this. Go find your safe space and get it *all* out.

This is what we call emotional honesty. And now that you're actually being honest with how you're feeling right now, you can enter into an honest dialogue with yourself to challenge whether your feelings align with truth. Examine your self-talk. Would your friends say these words about you? Is this how your younger self would speak to you today? Are these the words you're *really* choosing to define you?

To claim your calm on your worst day, you need to start with the most honest version of yourself. Only then can you begin to differentiate irrational thoughts from reality. And then it's up to you. One of the most beautiful things about your peace is that it is always available to you. There will never be a time when you reach for it and can't find it.

DESIGNATE YOUR SAFE SPACE

Becoming emotionally honest with yourself can be intense and vulnerable, so make sure you're set up for success. First, find a place that is totally yours, where you feel confident. Maybe this is a car, a garden bench, or your favorite chair. Consider conditions that make you feel your best—a playlist, a relaxing pose, a familiar scent. Have your safe space ready to go for the tough days that will inevitably come. Then enter your designated safe space, free of self-judgment and shame.

— AFFIRMATION —

I will be honest with negative feelings and not rush toward positivity.

Embrace Your Best No

D o you find yourself feeling overwhelmed and stressed because you've been taking on more than you can handle? Are you stretching yourself thinner and thinner in the name of keeping everyone around you happy?

Your daily responsibilities have the power to cause stress, anxiety, and burnout, so imagine what happens when you continue to take on more activities and responsibilities that *don't* belong to you. Hear this: Your worth is not measured by how much you do for others, and people whose approval is contingent on your burnout are not people you need approval from.

You can still be a kind, giving person who cares for others while caring for yourself, but the trick is to embrace your best no. Your best no isn't given out willy-nilly. It's given thoughtfully, carefully, and with consideration of feelings (yours as well as the person asking).

When you say yes to everyone around you, you're saying no to yourself. But when you say no to things that do not serve you, you are making room for an even greater, more enthusiastic yes.

I can stand firm in my boundaries.

DETERMINE YOUR NO

Take time today to write out your nonnegotiables and boundaries in the chief categories of your life. These are the rules you have set for your work life and relationships, and at its heart it's a list of what matters to you most. For example, is your bedtime routine nonnegotiable? Do you always take fifteen minutes before a meeting to prepare? Setting and keeping boundaries can feel difficult if you haven't practiced, but having them written out makes it possible to stand firm in them as you practice.

DAY 52

Pack Well, Bestie

How would you describe your packing style? Organized travelers have everything in its place. They've got the packing cubes, extra chargers, and outfits categorized by day. Disorganized travelers might open their suitcase and throw in as much as they can, sitting on it and hoping everything will fit. (We're in this second category, so trust us—*no shade* if this is you too!)

Apply this idea to your emotions and ask yourself: Are you someone who comes with mental packing cubes, or are you the cluttered pack rat in this situation? Are you taking on the burdens of others? Overstuffed and cluttered minds are a sign that you're carrying more than you were meant to. When you try to put that bag through baggage claim, you'll find that it weighs too much, and you will have to pay a fee. The fee is often your calm.

Are all these emotions serving you? It can feel tempting to continually pack in more, especially if you're feeling fearful about not being good enough, but there's only so much you can handle at once. Make a practice of naming and organizing your emotions, then let go of the ones that aren't yours to bear and note how much lighter your mind feels.

LIGHTEN YOUR LOAD

Today, take inventory of what you're carrying that doesn't belong to you. Taking on feelings and emotions for those around you, worrying about the future, even just stressing about the status of a coworker's project—these things are not yours to carry. Make the decision to let them go. Remind yourself that you can't lose what wasn't yours in the first place. Let them go and watch your stress and anxiety levels improve.

———— AFFIRMATION ————

I can let go of emotions that are not mine to bear.

DAY 53

What If This Goes Right?

Imagine you're at lunch with a friend and you start describing an event you're going to. It's an event you're very excited about. You tell this friend that you bought a new dress, and they respond by asking, "What if you look out of place? Are you sure you want to wear that?" You tell them you can't wait to meet some fun, new people, and they say, "Are you going to laugh? You laugh so loud. You know your laugh is weird, right?" You tell them you're excited about the restaurant, and they say, "What if you get food poisoning?"

If you actually know someone like this, you do *not* want to be friends with them. You're probably not surprised to hear this, but the "friend" in this scenario is named Anxiety. Anxiety wants to point out everything that could go wrong, so you'll need to speak up for yourself when it does. Combat the negative what-if thinking with positive what-if thinking. Instead of *What if this goes wrong?*, start thinking, *What if this goes right?* Balancing your emotions helps to ground you and gives you strength in the midst of anxiety.

I can speak positively over my situation.

GET BOTH SIDES OF THE STORY

When you're experiencing anxiety, it can feel natural to point out everything that could go wrong. Before stepping into a situation that you consider stressful, write a list of the things making you feel nervous. Then write a list of the things you feel excited about. Finally, write a list of the things that are both. The goal isn't to minimize negative emotions, but to find balance in them. You can find the positives, even among the things that make you nervous.

Return to Your Body

Have you ever had a particularly stressful day (or week or month) and thought to yourself, *When this is all over, I'm going to feel great*. You hoped that, at the end of it all, you'd feel reinvigorated and calm because you'd no longer be overwhelmed or overworked.

Mm-hmm, and how did that go?

Ever heard of a stress hangover? That feeling of exhaustion, fogginess, and inability to focus, even long after you've accomplished your work? Just as a regular hangover tells the story of the night before (bad karaoke, margaritas with friends), your body holds on to the story of your stress. You may not notice it right away, but over time you'll find that anxiety and stress can influence your physical health.

The good news is you can get better. You may not be able to take two painkillers, eat a greasy breakfast, and down a sports drink to get rid of this kind of hangover, but you *can* reclaim your health. Sometimes it's as simple as returning to your body, taking stock of where you're holding tension, and inviting relaxation.

CHECK IN WITH YOUR BODY

Take some time to find out where you hold tension. Lie on the floor and mentally scan your body, starting at the bottoms of your feet and moving up to the crown of your head. Wherever you notice tension, massage, stretch, or shake that part of your body. Let yourself feel heavy and send your breath into the areas that feel the most tense. Go as slow as you need, until each limb feels like it's sinking into the floor beneath you. When you're finished, rise slowly and sit up, rolling through one vertebra at a time.

AFFIRMATION

I will return to my body ✦ whenever ✦ my mind races.

DAY 55

Tell the Truth

I f you've been struggling with anxiety for any length of time, you've likely had thoughts similar to these:

Will I always be anxious?
This is just who I am now, I guess.
I don't know who I am if I'm not anxious.

Given enough time, your anxiety can feel synonymous with your very being. You don't remember the last time you *weren't* anxious. Then you start to wonder whether you're even able to function without this steady pace of fear because it's all you've known. Ground yourself in this truth today: You are not your anxious thoughts or your anxiety.

It's important in those moments of worry to remind yourself of who you are. You're a three-dimensional human with thoughts and feelings that don't revolve around your worry and fear. You have the capacity for peace and a hunger for stability. You can return to your breath and your body when you feel shaky. Then, equipped with the truth of who you are, you can beat back the voice in your head that tells you you'll always be anxious.

I am more · than my anxious · thoughts.

KNOW THYSELF

Who are you? You are not your anxious thoughts. It can be easy to forget this during a stressful time or when you're feeling anxious. Write down the truths of who you are. What do you like? What do you want most? Whom do you love, and who loves you? Where are your favorite places to be? Where are you most yourself? When do you feel at your best? Speak these truths over yourself; it is in them that your calm can be found.

DAY 56

Face the Facts

I f your boss puts a meeting on your calendar without warning, you may feel yourself losing your cool. Your mind races. *They didn't tell me about this meeting*, you think. *They must be angry with me*, you might assume. *I'm about to be reprimanded . . .* actually, *I'm probably going to be fired.* The panic begins. Suddenly, there is *no* chance your boss simply wants to grab a coffee or talk through a project. In these moments, your feelings feel like facts.

When you find yourself in a spiral of thoughts like these, think of yourself as a detective. (We also encourage a cool notepad and hat.) Investigate whether the statements you're telling yourself are really true. Can you support these statements with facts? Might there be other points of view?

This isn't to say you shouldn't trust what you're feeling. But the best thing you can do is slow down and gather more information. If your mind is rushing ahead of reality, you aren't doing yourself a service following it there. Stay present and define what you know and what you don't. Breathe, and trust that whatever happens next, you are calm and capable of managing it.

My feelings ✦
✦ are not facts.

BECOME A FACT COLLECTOR

Whatever you're feeling anxious about today, it's time to state the facts about that situation. Get a piece of paper and something to write with; then set a timer for five minutes. Create two columns: one for what you are feeling and one that states the facts of that situation. Start all the statements in the "feelings" column with "I feel," "I felt," or "I am feeling." Then write out the facts, objectively. Seeing them separated makes them easier to untangle.

Get Back to You

I just don't feel like myself." Whether these words were whispered or screamed aloud in our cars, we've all been there. And friend, it's the worst feeling. Burnout has a way of making us feel irritable, exhausted, disinterested, and even depressed. You may feel like you're walking around in a fog, trying to navigate your way back to the person who was once capable of peace and joy. You can feel very far away from who you are, what you like to do, and who you like to spend time with. You may find yourself acting out of character.

Here's our encouragement today: That person still exists within you! Celebrate all the facets of you. You are a complex person with likes, dislikes, interests that make you light up, opinions that make you feel angry, disappointments you've worked through, and joy you've felt. You know what activities, foods, and friends you love.

Developing a clear image of yourself away from the stress and worry helps you latch on to something when you're feeling down. Think about the truest, best version of you and keep that vision close. You are a wonder. Never forget that.

BREAK IN CASE OF EMERGENCY

Create a "break in case of emergency" protocol for the days you don't feel like yourself. Watch your favorite TV show, eat your favorite meal, spend time with close friends or family. Collect the things that remind you of who you truly are and that you enjoy. Have these ready when anxiety and stress make you feel disconnected from yourself.

AFFIRMATION

I know who I am, and I can always find myself.

DAY 58

Mind Your Business

Anxiety can make us a bit self-focused and not always in the most productive way. No judgment here. It's just that anxiety has a way of making us believe that everything is about us. For example, when you're walking into a party, you may be thinking about how you look, what other people think about what you're wearing, whether the people there will think you're funny, and whether you'll make friends. In reality, no one is thinking about you as much as *you* are thinking about you. And anyway, what people think about you is truly none of your business.

Worrying about what other people think is natural, but making other peoples' opinions worth something only interrupts your sense of calm and joy. Especially if they're people you don't really know or understand.

There will be people who love you, who dislike you, who don't get your sense of humor, who hate the way you dress. This is for certain. But you don't need to listen to them. Take stock of what *you* think, how *you'd* act. And you know what? Dare to enjoy it.

What other people think about me is none of my business.

KNOW WHAT YOU THINK

Your sense of calm and self-worth comes from within. On a piece of paper, write down the qualities that you like, not because other people admire them but because you like them. Write down what impresses you about yourself, not because of others being impressed. Develop an opinion of yourself and strive to be someone you like and would want to spend time with.

DAY 59

Seek Proof of the Positive

When you're nervous or worried, your brain seeks confirmation to validate how you're feeling.[34] You might turn to another person (or many others) and ask them what they think of the situation, search for more information on the internet, or overthink your decisions. It can sometimes be easier to see the negative than to focus on the positive. You are not a failure, you're human.

It's exhausting to look for the positives when your feelings are anything but. Ask yourself: *What would happen if I spent time looking for the bright side, rather than focusing on how worried I am?*

You may have your eye on a gray cloud that's blocking the sun, grumbling about its presence and feeling disappointment or annoyance, but when you open your eyes and zoom out on the issue, you can see that the cloud has a silver lining. Whether you have plenty of practice looking on the bright side of life or you find it a little difficult, use this as an opportunity to name these silver linings aloud. And hey, as a bonus, these musings may even encourage others around you.

iDENTIFY THE SILVER LININGS

Look back on some of the times you've felt the most anxious, worried, or fearful. Reflect on the good that came out of those situations. This can include things you learned about yourself or others, people you met when you pushed yourself outside of your comfort zone, experiences you might not have had. Practicing seeking out the silver linings can make you better at spotting them in real time.

—— **AFFIRMATION** ——

I will focus on the silver linings rather than the clouds.

We're Not Gonna Scroll (as Much) Anymore

Social media has opened us up to endless possibilities and connections. It makes it possible to keep in touch, learn, laugh, and relate with friends, family, and strangers. And those cute dog videos? Fab!

But along with all the positive aspects of social media, there are negatives. With an endless stream of content at your fingertips, there's immense temptation to stay plugged in, distracting you from where you are in the present. There's also the compulsion to share (and overshare), to comment and like, to overconsume, and worst of all, to compare yourself to others.

A surefire way to lose your joy and calm is to keep yourself glued to the phone and away from reality, as time spent online can often lead to comparing your life to others—both people you know and people you don't—creating envy and anxiety where there was contentment.

I am doing the best that I can, and that is enough.

TAKE A SOCIAL MEDIA BREAK

Comparing yourself to the people gracing your social media feeds has the potential to steal your joy by making you feel like you're not doing enough. Scrolling (and scrolling and scrolling) through everyone's highlight reel is like holding the door open for anxiety and inviting it in. Look, we need some moderation, friends! What would it look like to take a break and create some parameters? Start with a few hours if a whole day doesn't seem possible, but eventually, work your way up to a day or entire weekend free of social media.

DAY 61

Prepare for Joy

When was the last time you belly laughed? Like really laughed and couldn't stop? We're talking milk-up-the-nose kind of laughter—the kind that hurts the muscles in your face. Humor is one of the most efficient ways to interrupt the downward spiral and put you on the path to calm. Laughter and fear are like oil and water: They do not mix.

Joy can feel far away when you're struggling to figure out how to keep going, but you can be confident that your joy is always waiting for you, ready to be summoned at any moment. Rest in the fact that you have known joy before, and you will know it once again.

You can prepare for stressful moments by becoming curious about what brings you joy. Love a comedy special? Some talking-cat videos? An old movie from your childhood? Watching your kids attempt a new craft? Spend time with yourself and be honest about the things you love. Once you can name them, you'll be able to return to them as touchstones when life gets hard.

MAKE A HAPPY LIST

Make a list of ten (or more) things that make you truly happy: memories, songs, people, or things that instantly bring a smile to your face. Whenever you feel your anxiety bubbling up to the surface, go to your happy list. Turn on your favorite song and dance, text that person to let them know you're thinking of them, sit and reminisce about a pleasant memory. If ever it feels hard to conjure up joy, return to the list.

——— **AFFIRMATION** ———

I have known ✦ joy before, and I will know it again.

✦

DAY 62

Research Your Rest

Most of us who experience anxiety are very curious people. From looking up medical symptoms online to deep dives on social media, we're going to guess you have plenty of practice gathering information. So instead of putting that skill to use to confirm and exacerbate your anxiety, it's time to use it to make a change. Your subject today? Your rest.

Rest comes in many different forms. Not only physical but also mental, emotional, social, creative, sensory, and spiritual rest. Become curious with yourself about which kinds of rest you prioritize and which you may be excluding right now. There's no right way to rest or perfect balance to achieve—only you have the self-knowledge of what balance feels like for you. But if you're finding you're burnt-out and haven't been able to access your calm lately, ask yourself which of these areas may be lacking.

You have the authority to reset your rest today. Tap into what you need, and reclaim your right to prioritize yourself. When you rest, the rest of life will fall into place.

I am in control of my routine; my routine does not control me.

PERFORM A "SLEEP STUDY"

Research your rest throughout the week. Note in your journal or on your phone when you experience one of the forms of rest listed above, and keep a running tally. Write briefly about how you feel after each restful activity. Repeat throughout the week, noting how your rest ebbs and flows. If you notice you're completely lacking rest in one area of your life, don't fret. With this new awareness, you have the power to make a change, should you so choose.

Take the Easy Way

D on't take the easy way out." You might've heard this phrase before, perhaps meant as encouragement to help you push through a tough time. There are plenty of times when it's rewarding to challenge yourself, but there are also times when the task you face requires surrender instead. In moments when you find yourself gripped with fear, it's okay to take the easy road.

Do not confuse the *easy way* with *giving up*. The two could not be more different. Giving up looks like throwing your hands up and abandoning yourself. We're not suggesting that. What *are* we suggesting? We like to think of the "easy way" as an openhandedness, recognizing that some things are simply outside of our control.

When you recognize what's not in your control, you'll be more equipped to maneuver what *is* in your control. From this posture of surrender, you may find more clarity to strategize about what you *can* change. It may be frustrating to realize some things are outside your control, and you may not meet the idealized expectations you have for yourself. Still, keep it easy. Let go of what you can and home in on your capacity, your capability, and your commitment to simply do your best.

I can take the easy way in times of overwhelm.

TAKE THE EASY WAY

Identify one way you can take the easy way today. Ask yourself if there's a particular issue or situation that keeps entering your thoughts. Not everything deserves your complete and total attention. The key to calm is determining where to put your time and energy, and focusing on problems outside your control is not one of them. Identify one nagging task or area of life that you can surrender today, recognizing that not everything will go your way and that is okay.

Enter the Ring

Have you ever watched a boxing match? Two people go toe to toe, punching and jabbing, landing punches, swinging and missing. Eventually, they retreat to their separate corners of the ring, where they sit down, mop the sweat from their brows, get advice from their coaches, and refresh themselves for the next round.

In the moments after they replenish their stores, the boxers need to make another choice to get into the ring. Starting the match is the easy part (though it doesn't always feel like it), but stepping back into the ring for the next round can be more difficult.

Experiencing stress or anxiety every day can feel like a boxing match. Some days you feel healthy and powerful; other days it takes longer to get back up from a particularly vicious round.

No matter what you're experiencing today, hear this: You are not powerless against your anxiety. You can step into the ring and take it on, jabbing back at lies with truth. You can also reserve your strength for the next round, calling on previously learned tactics to ground yourself and take hold of your calm.

THROW SOME PUNCHES

Your calm is worth fighting for. Today, throw some physical punches at your anxiety. Make a fist and throw a punch into the air. As you do, speak truth and confidence over yourself and your situation. Choose from some of the mantras we have used already. Pairing physical movement with emotional intention can help solidify it in your mind.[35] When your anxiety tells you a lie today, fight back with the truth.

— AFFIRMATION —

I can fight back my anxious thoughts.

Mistakes Teach Us Grace

When a toddler tips over a cup of milk, you don't scream at them as if they've done real damage. They're new here and still learning how to experience the world around them. Instead of yelling, you help them clean up their mess and explain ways to avoid making another one in the future. For some reason, as we get older, we begin to treat mistakes like a *huge* deal. Yet we are *also* humans inhabiting today for the very first time. Mistakes are inevitable.

You may fear making mistakes and all their repercussions. That's okay and natural. But no matter what your anxious mind says, mistakes are incredibly useful tools— once you get over your fear of making them. When you do something incorrectly, you learn how to do better next time. Better yet? You also learn the power of accepting grace and being gracious with others. You have more practice keeping your calm. Mistakes are a sign that you are growing and learning, progressing toward the higher, better version of you. So give yourself some space and grace, and observe your mistakes from this new frame.

I can learn and grow ✦
✦ from my mistakes.

GROW THROUGH IT

On a sheet of paper, draw a flower with five petals. In the center of your flower, write the mistake you feel that you made. (Sometimes you can convince yourself you've made a mistake when the opposite is true. Just don't be too hard on yourself.) On the petals of the flower, write five things you learned from your mistake or opportunities for growth. This takes the focus off the mistake and onto your growth.

Protect Your Calm

Imagine your mind as a house. Every night, you lock up before going to bed. You check the doors and windows to be sure your home is secure. Maybe you even have a security system that makes you feel more at peace. Nothing is allowed to pass through those entry points, unless you let it. You are in control.

Stress and anxiety may make you feel powerless at times, but you can build a fortress around your peace and keep it secure. So what kinds of techniques might you incorporate into your "security system" to keep out anxiety and protect your calm?

For starters, check your body and breath; start here to maintain regulation. Even, easy breathing is the first line of defense for your calm state of being. Then, move on to your thought life. Do you have a go-to list of mantras and truths that you can return to? Memorize them and hold them tight. These are your lines of defense against the hard times. *You* have the power to protect your calm.

I can fortify my calm.

CHECK YOUR LOCKS

Scan your body for tension, noting where you're feeling it and releasing it as you go. Think of every little release as a lock falling into place, signaling security to your mind and body. Take an inventory of your day, noting the moments you felt nervous or overwhelmed, and look forward to tomorrow, devising a plan and setting intentions for how you'll handle your stress and anxiety. Feel the locks click securely shut as you remind yourself you have the power to protect your calm.

Follow Your Voice

There is a voice inside you whose job is to tell you the truth. Sometimes it shouts and sometimes it whispers. It's the voice that soothes and regulates and tells you everything will be all right. It's the voice that tells you about your dignity. The voice that cares for you and believes you are good and worthy of good things. Call that voice intuition, call it your gut, but hear this: That voice is worth listening to. The voice that believes in you and speaks kind things over you? That's the truth-teller.

Your circumstances may be disorienting, making you feel frantic, confused, and burnt-out, which can then make you doubt the good and kind voice inside your head. Has it been hard for you to hear it? Have you lost trust in it? Whatever the case, the good news is that it's always available to you. Developing a relationship with this voice can help you understand yourself, offer you a better view of reality, and banish the anxious voice in your head that often contradicts it.

TALK IT OUT

Spend the day talking to yourself. This can be out loud or simply inside your mind. Narrate your thoughts about your day and the truths of your circumstances. Keep it positive, avoiding negative self-talk and acting as your own biggest cheerleader. And most important: When your inner voice is kind to you, believe it. Making a practice of this will make it easier to hear this voice when your anxiety tries to drown it out.

Everything will be okay.

DAY 68

Find Your Confidence

Think of the most confident person you know. Maybe this is a person in your life or even a character in your favorite show. Conjure them in your mind at their most poised. What are they doing? How do they carry themselves? What emotions do you feel when you picture them this way?

If you asked this person how they became so confident, how do you think they'd respond? Chances are—if they're being honest with you—they would describe times when they felt scared. Maybe when they failed. But then they'd tell you how they persevered and kept trying anyway because true confidence is earned. The most confident and successful person you know likely didn't start that way. They chose to keep learning and growing, even when afraid.

You don't need to be great to feel confident. You just need courage to persevere, even when you're scared. Courage to silence that voice in your head listing all that could go wrong and instead listen to the part of yourself that wonders what could go right. As you practice courage, you'll find that your fear starts to melt away to make space for joy.

BE BAD AT SOMETHING

What are some areas of your life where you've left your confidence unexplored? Pick an activity, any activity. Tennis, embroidery, watercolor, gardening—anything you have been thinking of doing but have been afraid of failing at. Or maybe choose that small, stressful task at work that you've been avoiding. Whatever it is, commit to doing it. Just start! It might bring you anxiety at first, but you might also be great! Either way, you'll walk away more confident than you were yesterday.

Confidence is available to me when I choose to do hard things.

Check Your Foundation

When builders construct a house, they first lay down a foundation—arguably one of the most important features in your home. It provides a base so that everything else upon it can withstand wind, storms, earthquakes, and more. The foundation provides the solidity needed to stand tall.

When a storm of feelings rages around you, you may start to wonder whether you're built to withstand that kind of onslaught. Your "house" feels like it was built on sand, sinking into the ground, or on the edge of a cliff and in danger of falling off. Your anxious thoughts can often trick you into believing that your foundation has crumbled beneath you into a million pieces.

In these moments, check in with yourself: What are your guiding principles? The beliefs that are core to you? Recite them aloud, if that's helpful. Ground yourself in your body, returning to your breath. Now you can stand with your feet planted, knowing you possess the strength necessary to weather the anxiety you're feeling. You're not in quicksand, nor is the ground simply going to disappear. You are on solid ground; your foundation is firm because you built it.

I can stand firm on solid ground.

STAND FIRM

Stand up straight with your feet shoulder-width apart, preferably barefoot. Let your feet connect with the floor. Notice how solid it is. Allow yourself to feel supported by the ground. It does not sway or shift; it will not simply disappear. Remind yourself that you are always on solid ground, even when it feels rocky or slippery. Repeat this activity as necessary.

DAY 70

Dream of Tomorrow

C ontrary to what you may have thought when you picked up this book, reading it does not guarantee you will never again have another bad, stressful, anxious day. In fact, the only guarantee is that you *will* have bad days (it's only human), but you'll also have new tools to handle them.

As cliché as it sounds, you can't have good days without a few bad ones. If every single one of your days was perfect, you'd never know when one was truly incredible. Having not-so-great or even downright terrible days gives you some perspective to appreciate the days where everything goes your way.

Here's the truth about bad days: They end. And at the end of those days, you get to close your eyes, fall asleep, and wake up to another opportunity. So if you're dreading today because yesterday was terrible or if you've just had a hard day and aren't feeling hopeful about tomorrow, it's time to take ownership. What are some things you can do, places you can go, or people you can see to be sure this day is better than the last?

CREATE A BETTER TOMORROW

Remind yourself there is always tomorrow. Keep a list (in your phone or journal) of the positive things you will do tomorrow to make it better than today. Wake up a little early to enjoy your coffee in peace, schedule happy hour with pals, or sign up for a workout class. Work on making tomorrow better, rather than ruminating on the ways today didn't go your way.

—————— **AFFIRMATION** ——————

At the end of the day, there is always tomorrow.

DAY 71

Show Yourself Grace

I magine competing in a sport at a professional level without ever having practiced. Not only do you possess little skill, but you're unsure of the rules, and you keep running the wrong way on the court. Stacked up against people with a *ton* of experience, you may feel bad about yourself, until you remember: *I just got here! I'm doing the best I can!*

You deserve this grace, every day. Anxiety and stress go hand in hand with low self-esteem. You may be overly critical of yourself, feeling hopeless to learn something new or lacking confidence.

Remember, life is a sport you did not train for and are learning on the spot. You may feel like you're *really* good at it, or you might take some time to develop your skills. Or maybe you've experienced some success, so now you're being challenged to play at a higher level. The most important thing you can do is have grace and compassion for yourself so that you can learn and grow in a safe place. There is calm to be found, even as you're doing hard things, if you choose to be compassionate toward yourself. This self-compassion is the secret to leveling up!

I can show myself grace and be proud of myself along the way.

LEAVE A REVIEW

When a restaurant or business has excellent service or when you purchase a product that you are super impressed with, you are encouraged to leave a review. You shout out everything you loved about your experience and give kudos where they are due. Today, leave yourself a positive review. Write out what you loved about yourself and your day, and show gratitude for the moments you handled with grace.

Stretch Your Imagination

Raise your hand if, when faced with a stressful situation, you immediately start to imagine what could go wrong. You're not alone. Whether you're put into a stressful situation or you entered one of your own free will, when you feel your control over a situation slipping, it is a natural response to grasp for control. One of the ways you do this is by imagining the worst-case scenario and beginning to plot your way out of it. This can feel comforting in the moment but in the long run can reap unhealthy consequences.

Being prepared is totally great. Most of us have a spare tire in the trunk of our cars in case a tire goes flat or a flashlight in our bedside tables in case the lights go out. But there is a moment when preparation turns to catastrophizing, and soon you're focusing on the worst-case scenario even when it's unlikely to happen.

To combat this thought pattern, you'll need to lean on your imagination. Rather than imagining what could go wrong, create excitement and expectation around what can (and will) go right.

GET DRAMATIC (FOR YOUR GOOD)

Uncertainty is the one thing you can be certain of. Uncertainty is not an inherently bad thing, but when you struggle with anxiety and stress, it's often associated with negative outcomes. Today, ask yourself what would happen if you allowed yourself to imagine a positive outcome instead. Be extreme. Instead of asking "What if it goes wrong?" ask "What if it goes right?" Instead of spiraling down into the negative, allow the possibility of positivity to propel you upward.

—— AFFIRMATION ——

✦ I can visualize a less ✦ stressful day.

DAY 73

Savor the Sunsets

We know it's cliché, but really—does it ever get old? Every day, the sun rises in the east and sets in the west. Unchanging in its constancy but varied in its beauty. No two sunsets are alike—the light reflecting an array of colors into the sky, depending on the night and the weather conditions.

Sunsets remind us of two things. The first is to be present; you won't see the same sunset twice, so savor it. The second is there will always be another. It may not be the same, but the sun and sky give you plenty of chances to marvel at their beauty. If you miss one sunset, another one is twenty-four hours away.

There's something comforting in this consistency. Even if you don't get to see the sun setting every single night, you know it happened. You know it will happen again—even when hidden by clouds. The sun will set, then it will rise, and in that time between, you can find peace knowing a new day is coming. When you're feeling out of control or stressed, remember that every day is another chance.

There is always another chance.

WATCH A SUNSET

Tonight, weather permitting, head outside and simply watch the sun disappear behind the horizon. Sit in stillness and observe it closely. Name the colors as you watch the light interact with the clouds and dye them pinks and purples. The sun rose and set today; there is no question about it. It will rise and set tomorrow. You get to bear witness to the passing of time and accept that there will always be another chance.

Rest, Reset, Remind

The age-old advice given to everyone with an electronic device on the fritz—"Turn it off and then turn it back on"—is often the exact advice you should give yourself when feeling burnt-out.

There will be times when you need to perform the same reset on yourself when you are feeling lost, aimless, or otherwise disoriented because of stress or anxiety. It offers a chance to rest, reset, and remind yourself so that you can start tomorrow differently from how today ended.

Part of the rebooting process is not just resting but reconnecting with your *why*—the reasons you're doing, well, anything. For example, Why do you go to work? To pay your mortgage, to afford dinner with friends, to satisfy your passions, to provide for your family?

Resetting and reminding yourself of your purpose helps to put your life into perspective so you can find steadiness and focus. With this in view, you'll feel more like you—capable and determined to take on today.

HIT THE RESET

Today, sit down and write out the why to a task you're not looking forward to. Why do you go to work? Why do you meal prep? Why do you clean your house? The answer is often to benefit yourself or those you love in some way. If you find you have activities or responsibilities that you don't know the reason for, or that don't benefit you, try to find the positive. If you can't, reevaluate whether they serve you at all.

AFFIRMATION

I can reset and reorient myself when I am feeling aimless.

DAY 75

The Bestie Mindset

ave you ever had the joy to reunite with a friend or family member after not seeing one another for a while? You know the smile on their face when they see you, busting into the room and running over to give you a hug? Those old, good friends that make you feel at home—there's nothing like them. Get a really clear picture in your head of that loving person in your life. Imagine them as clearly as you can.

Next time you're feeling tough on yourself, we want you to imagine that person sitting beside you, cheering you on. Imagine the things they would tell you about yourself, and practice extending that same kindness and compassion toward yourself. Maybe they say things like:

> "You are more than able to do this. You are amazing!"
> "I know you're scared right now, but you are not
>   alone."
> "Don't be too hard on yourself, okay?"
> "You are allowed to try and fail at hard things."

By changing the way you talk to yourself when no one is listening, you don't feed stress and anxiety, and you take control of your thoughts in a loving, nurturing way.

I am worthy
✦ of happiness
and peace. ✦

BE YOUR OWN BFF

Write down a specific negative belief that's been nagging you lately. Now pretend your best friend, sibling, or partner said this about themselves. What would you say? Jot it down. Now, speak this positive response over yourself out loud. (We promise, it's more powerful if you really say it.) Start writing a positive story about yourself and your anxiety.

DAY 76

Keep Dreaming Forward

Remember when you were a kid and used to dream of what you'd be when you grew up? Astronaut, actor, veterinarian? What did you want and expect? Are there any parts of your dreams that have stayed the same? What's different? Chances are, your dreams have shifted throughout the years, but there's something to be learned about yourself from that childhood wish.

Let's get back to how fun it was to dream, before your sense of obligation set in. Before worry and fear started to drive your imagination. Before embarrassment set in and before you worried about pleasing other people. Back when things felt easy.

Yes, you're older and wiser now, and the responsibilities you bear are worth consideration. But ask yourself: *Are my worries standing in the way of who I want to be? Is my fear of failure preventing me from even getting started or making the changes I need?* Rekindle that childlike, reckless imagination. Your dreams will likely continue to morph over time, and that's okay. The point is, you're not going to let fear stand in your way.

DARE TO DREAM

There is ease to be found when you're living in alignment with your dreams. Grab a note card and scribble one word of what you want the most—something that is at least somewhat in your control. It can be anything: Move to a new city, ask that guy on a date, pursue a new career path, book a vacation. Put this note card in a place you pass by every day. And every day, take stock: Is this still what you want? If so, make a small tick mark on the card, agreeing you still want it. And then ask: How can I nudge my way closer today to making that a reality?

—— **AFFIRMATION** ——

I will pursue my dream, ✦ even when ✦ afraid.

DAY 77

Dwell in the Positives

What was the last kind thing you said to yourself? When you are feeling anxious or stressed, it is common to get caught up in patterns of negative thinking, especially about yourself. It usually starts small: *I can't believe I did that!* or *I am not good enough to do this!* But if you're not aware, those initial negative thoughts can spiral into thoughts of unworthiness, loneliness, and sadness.

For every negative thought, ask yourself if there's a more helpful, positive thought to replace it with. For example, if you're thinking, *I'm never going to get a promotion*, pause and reframe it to *I am qualified, and I do my best to advocate for myself or ask for help*.

Make yourself at home in the positives because these kinds of words and phrases are going to define this new era of you. You are choosing to be a person who extends compassion to themselves. You choose joy, not because it necessarily makes sense but because this is who you are. You choose to love yourself no matter what. And we think that's wonderful, y'all.

I am in control of the words I speak over myself.

COUNTER THE NEGATIVES

Shifting out of negativity into positivity is a lifelong journey, but you've got this! Start the day right by writing a truth about yourself that counters whatever negative thought pattern you're stuck in. You can do this on the bathroom mirror with a dry-erase marker or leave Post-its somewhere you'll see them.

They can look like this:

I am qualified.

I am loved.

I am beautiful.

I am doing my best.

I am where I'm meant to be.

We believe in you. Will you?

A Tidy Mind

O n days when it feels like your mind is stuffed with too many thoughts, it's important to take some time to tidy up. Just like an unkempt room, our minds require regular cleaning so we can better organize how we really feel. An orderly mind allows you to reflect with clarity, enabling you to make better choices and embrace your calm era for the long haul.

We like to take the kitchen-counter approach: A little bit every day goes a long way! Don't let those pesky, intrusive thoughts sit there for too long. Get them out of your head and onto some paper. No doubt, there will be valid worries and fears to jot down, but take special note when you start to talk negatively about *yourself*. Disliking your circumstances is one thing, but disliking yourself? That would be doing you a *total* disservice.

If you ever notice you're starting to speak negatively toward yourself, stop the cycle by walking around the room and getting some sunlight on your body, if you can. Connect back to your body and to the world around you, remembering that you are *good* and *capable* and *worthy* of peace.

BREATHE A NEW WAY

In yoga, pranayama is a breathing practice that helps to calm the mind and reset the thoughts.[36] Find a comfortable seated position. Gently close your eyes and take one slow inhale followed by an exhale. Then place your right thumb over your right nostril. Inhale slowly through the left nostril, imagining the breath coming upward along the left side of your body. Then, place your right pinky finger over your left nostril, exhaling through the right side. Now reverse the trajectory—inhaling through the right and exhaling through the left. Do as many rounds as needed to allow your thoughts to slow and your body to relax.

------ **AFFIRMATION** ------

I will redirect ✦ my thoughts to ones that ✦ serve me.

Honor Your Fear

No matter how practiced you become at finding your calm, there is still going to be some hard stuff in your life. No matter how much you prepare, you're going to fall short of expectations. And that will hurt.

After experiencing something difficult, you may try to avoid negative emotions at all costs and guard yourself against difficult situations—sometimes to the point that you stop pursuing what you love. While it would be great to live stress-free, you can't Bubble Wrap your life to avoid anxiety. Although it may feel like you're protecting yourself, a fully insulated life is just another form of fear. (And spoiler: Probably not going to work anyway.)

Don't let fear hold you back from chasing what you want. Hard things will come, and it's natural to experience some negative emotions when they do. Don't shame yourself for that. (If you haven't caught on yet, we don't do shame here.) The goal isn't to avoid anxiety entirely. The goal is to normalize it, honor it, and find a way to keep moving forward toward your desired highest self.

I will not ✦ let anxiety make me ✦ guarded.

DO WHAT YOU CAN (AND NOTHING MORE)

Take sixty seconds to list the things you want most. As you go, make a second column, noting what emotions you feel, remembering that any emotion is okay. Then pick the desire that feels the most vulnerable to you—the one that stirs the most fear—and write it at the top of the next page. Take sixty more seconds, jotting down every obstacle that stands in your way. (Yep, we hate this part too—keep going!) Now circle any obstacle over which you have some control. Whatever you circled, therein lies your power. Do one thing this next week to address that obstacle.

DAY 80

Make Good Habits

Your day is made up of many different habits you've made, whether consciously or not. Brushing your teeth, making your coffee, making dinner—these are all habits you've stuck to. Here's the good news: You've kept up your good habits and turned them into a routine.

The bad news is you may have also accidentally allowed some bad habits to sneak into your life, which may be leaving you feeling regretful and more stressed. Bad habits like mindlessly scrolling on your phone before bed, not getting enough sleep, hitting snooze on your alarm, or ordering takeout "just one more time" during the week. Over time, these habits make their way into daily life and slowly steal your calm.

No more! We're taking back your calm! For every undesirable habit you've established, you can replace it with one that's better for reaching your personal goal of finding your calm. Swap out the scroll for a quick yoga flow. Exchange that fourth cup of coffee for a bright and sparkly lemonade. Switch out that third episode on television for a short, low-impact workout. You made these habits, and you have the focus it takes to make new ones.

STACKING IS THE SECRET

Take advantage of the habits you already have by layering others on top of them, turning them into groups. To make it simple, take a habit you need and then add on to it a habit you'd like to have or do. For example, if you make your coffee every morning, add on the habit of meditating while you do. What are one or two new habits you can start grouping with established habits to promote more calm in your life?

—— AFFIRMATION ——

I can create helpful habits ✦ to alleviate my stress.

Follow Light

Stress can feel like you're burning a candle at both ends. When you're ultra-productive, you may be giving off twice as much light as you normally would, but that light will extinguish twice as fast. In the end, all you're left with is a burnt wick.

Your body is limited, and we want you to remember this is good and normal. Your limitations are a reminder that you are human. You have needs. And you deserve to have your needs met.

Take note of signs you may be burning out.[37] Unable to sleep? Change in appetite? The things you love don't feel as joyful anymore? These are red flags, friend! We are *not* going to let you lose your light. We love the way you shine.

When you feel on the verge of burnout, we're going to encourage you to press pause—even if that means you disappoint someone. Take a day and find things that light you up: the people you love, activities you find joy in, and practices that bring you peace. Chase the goodness in your life. Remind yourself that it exists, both within you and around you.

I am committed to protecting my brightness.

LET THE LIGHT IN

Start your day with sunshine. Doing so helps to regulate your circadian rhythm, giving you more energy in the morning and helping you sleep better at night.[38] It's also a total mood booster.[39] You can head outside or simply open your curtains and bask in the sunshine for a minute or two. If you live somewhere where sunshine is in short supply, consider investing in a light therapy lamp that mimics the light from the sun.

DAY 82

Invite Others In

Anxiety, depression, burnout, and stress are extremely common, so why is it that we hide these struggles from each other? Whether it's continuing to post on social media as if nothing is wrong or delivering the classic "I'm fine!" response when asked how we're doing, it's common to ignore the anxiety-shaped elephant in the room in the name of not "burdening" others.

Your anxiety wants you all alone. It wants you isolated. Peace, joy, and calm want you to be supported, loved, and cared for. They flourish in community.

Your fears, worries, and anxieties do not make you too complicated or messy. It's good to need other people. Share your thoughts and fears with your loved ones. You are not a burden to those who love you. You may have spent a lot of time isolating yourself to keep others from seeing your messy parts, but no more. Step into the light and invite others to see your imperfections. They do not make you weak. Just the very act of sharing them proves your courage.

✦ I can lean on people I love ✦ without guilt.

MAKE A DATE

Call a close friend or family member and ask them to join you for an activity. Take a walk, go out to eat, go to a museum—whatever you'd both like. Use that time together to remind yourself that the ones who love and care about you want to know what you are going through. Be honest with them about what is making you anxious or causing you stress, and encourage them to be honest as well.

DAY 83

Seek Out Your Senses

As you are probably aware, your senses of sight, touch, sound, taste, and smell do a lot to carry you through the spaces you inhabit. They work together, and when one sense is impaired, the others will work even harder to compensate. Think of each sense as your own little superpower, offering you information about the world around you so that you can form thoughts and opinions.

Anxiety and stress can do a good job of trapping you inside a thought-spiral focused on the past or future. This can make you feel disoriented and disconnected from reality. In these moments, tap into those sensory superpowers to bring you back to the present. You have a good, beautiful, wonderful physical body—pulsing with energy. All you must do is bring awareness to it.

This is why it is suggested that you taste a sour candy or hold on to an ice cube when you're anxious or feel panic.[40] A jolt to the system can cue your senses to focus on what's real and bring you back to the present. Your senses have the ability to break your thought patterns and bring you back to what is real, true, and tangible.[41]

GET BACK TO YOUR SENSES

When you are anxious, trust your senses to ground you.[42] A common technique is naming five things you can see, four things you can touch, three things you can hear, two things you can smell, and one thing you can taste. Remember this by counting down: five, four, three, two, one. This exercise will connect you to the world around you and keep your mind from focusing on your anxious thoughts.

—————— **AFFIRMATION** ——————

⋆ I can rely on my senses ⋆ to ground me.

DAY 84

You're Worth Celebrating

Observing a toddler feels a lot like watching them perform a one-person show. No matter what they do or how they do it, we like to applaud them! And that cute little grin on their face when we do? This is what we live for!

When we were young, everything we did was a celebration. First steps, first words, first dance recital, first day of school—the people around us made a *big* deal about the strides we were making. They celebrated some things because we did them for the first time, others because we did them even though they were new (and maybe even frightening) experiences for us. But at some point, this celebration stopped (or at least happened far, far less often).

Though you've mastered talking and walking, you are *still* making strides in your life. You are still doing things for the first time, even when it's difficult or frightening. But when was the last time you felt *celebrated* for something other than a birthday, wedding, or baby shower? Celebrating your everyday accomplishments (or even the big, important ones) with family, friends, or on your own gives you confidence to continue.

I can celebrate my successes.

TAKE TIME TO CELEBRATE

Set a list of realistic goals for yourself. Choose goals that feel doable in the next few months, like sticking to a gym routine, making your coffee at home for an entire month, or trying a new art class. Place a few goodies in a storage container and pull one out every time you achieve a goal on your list. Then remember to celebrate them. Every time you reach a goal, make yourself a cocktail or mocktail, open a prize, and make yourself feel special.

DAY 85

Sometimes That's All You Can Do

There will always be more to do. Dance recitals, house-sitting, building that piece of furniture, polishing that presentation one more time . . . In the pursuit of perfection, so many of us fall into the trap of saying yes, until we find ourselves snippy and burnt-out. In the name of ambition and progress, we may push past our limits and do harm to our minds and bodies over and over. And we think you deserve better than that!

Part of your healing and finding your calm will depend on you defining your thresholds and learning to express gratitude for them. Instead of being frustrated you can't *do more*, adopt a view that your limits—mental, physical, and emotional—are actually *good.* When your body is sending you signals that you're tired and burnt-out, what would it look like to express a spirit of gratitude toward yourself?

Honor your humanity by accepting that you need rest. Take pride that you are doing your best—and that might mean disappointing others. Take care of yourself and notice how much more present and available you are in your day-to-day life.

RECONSIDER RESPONSIBILITIES

Sit down and write out your daily and weekly responsibilities at work and at home. Note which ones you took on willingly, which you do begrudgingly, which you do because it is expected of you, and which you do because you didn't know how to say no. Reconsider each. Ask yourself which you must do and which you can delegate. Which you can say no to and which you would love to do. Rework your responsibilities so they work for you.

I do not need ✦ to take on more than ✦ I can handle.

BODY

DAY 86

Putting Yourself First

If you've ever flown on an airplane, you've heard the directive that, in the event of an emergency, you should put on your own oxygen mask first and then help those around you. Even before helping your kids! That's because if you don't take care of yourself first, you could end up passing out, and then you're of no help to yourself or others.

There will be no in-flight announcement or oxygen mask dropping from the ceiling today, but you should still practice putting yourself first. Here's what it could look like: Instead of coming home from work and immediately cooking dinner and getting the kids ready for bed, take five minutes to yourself in the car to listen to your favorite song or finish a podcast. Or rather than continuing to work late into the night, set a boundary and turn off your work phone.

When you take care of yourself first, you become a different person. You feel happier, healthier, and able to help others without becoming exhausted. Remember, there is no glory in wearing yourself thin. These intentional little steps along the way can connect you back to yourself and give you the energy you need to sustain for the long haul through the busy stages of life.

I can practice self-care and put myself first.

GO FOR THE GOOD STUFF

Set aside time today for self-care. Self-care can look like preparing your favorite lunch, doing an exercise you love, relaxing in a bath, reading a book, or going for a walk. It's about meeting your needs first and nurturing yourself. This may not feel natural for you at first, if you're always putting others' needs before yours, but take the time to try. It may feel so good that it leads to a more intentional self-care practice.

Silence Your Biggest Critic

D o you find that you're particularly self-critical when you're feeling overloaded by responsibilities or inundated with anxious thoughts? *Especially* when you're stressed? When you're not paying attention, self-doubt, disappointment, and self-deprecation slip through to remind you of all the things you're actually doing wrong. Sound familiar?

Negative self-talk isn't a harmless action. You may think it is, but in the long term it can make you feel even more anxious and wreak havoc on your self-esteem. Say enough "not so bad" things about yourself over time, and you'll start to believe them. And after all this good work, we're not going back to that! Nuh-uh.

No one hired you to be your biggest critic. You didn't even interview for that job. No one asked you to place judgments on yourself every day. It is not your responsibility to analyze (and overanalyze) things you've done or are doing. You are allowed to be kind to yourself (in fact, it's encouraged), so you can meet yourself with compassion and calm, rather than judgment.

I am capable, and I like myself.

CHOW DOWN ON A COMPLIMENT SANDWICH

While it would be amazing if you could simply stop criticizing yourself, it may not be possible to break the habit right away. So start a new one. Anytime you feel like you're about to criticize yourself, make a compliment sandwich: Tell yourself one nice thing about yourself, then the criticism, then another nice thing. Sandwich the critical feedback between compliments to ensure that you stay balanced in how you talk to yourself.

DAY 88

Show Yourself Some Love

Have you ever considered how wonderful your body is? Think of the walk you took yesterday with the help of your legs, or the meal you cooked with your arms and hands. Think of the book you read using your eyes, or the music you listened to with your ears. Your body physically carries you through every step of your life. That is something to be grateful for.

Maybe this kind of self-gratitude and focus isn't something you're comfortable with yet. Maybe you've been conditioned to point out your flaws, rather than celebrate yourself. Today, do your best to express gratitude to all the wonderful things that make you *you*. Yes, all the physical achievements of how you move through the world. But also the less tangible ones—like how you always learn your waiter's name. The way you make others laugh. How well you listen to your friends who are sad. You are smart and wonderful, and darn it, *we like you.*

If you're stuck in a cycle of focusing on your flaws, shift your attention and embrace who you are, thankful that this is the life you get to live and the beautiful body you get to do it in. You are magnificent. Don't forget it.

THANK YOURSELF

Your body and your mind have the incredible task of carrying you through the world, and they deserve some credit. Look at yourself in the mirror. Scan your body, starting from your toes, and tell your body "thank you" for carrying you through each day. Then look yourself in the eyes and name one thing you're great at. You are good, and you deserve to be celebrated.

— AFFIRMATION —

I don't need to be perfect; I just need to be me.

A Breath of Peace

O n days when your sense of calm feels far away, trust that you have done the work to find it again. You have the power to find your way back to the less anxious, less stressed version of yourself that you've worked hard to pursue.

Return to your breath, because your breath is always a lifeline back to the truest version of you. Remember that hard times are guaranteed to come, and in the same breath, remember that life will not always be this way. You are capable of facing today, and even when things don't go how you expect, you are powerful and grounded. You have what it takes to breathe through whatever comes your way because you know your worth.

Every time you return to your breath, you are proclaiming that you trust yourself and your body to carry you through. Here, connected with your body, cultivate the peace you need. It never left you, and it never will.

A CLEANSING MEDITATION

Find a comfortable position and close your eyes. Imagine yourself in a sea of blue. Notice the speed of your breath. Then, with your next inhale, imagine breathing in some of the blue air, filling your lungs and allowing your belly to expand. Imagine the color blue filling your body, dancing and swirling into each of your extremities. Then exhale a cleansing breath and imagine every worry leaving your body. Repeat as needed, until you sense your worries are outside of you. To finish, hold your hand over your heart, imagining a small glow coming from within. This is your peace; let it radiate through your entire body as you approach your day.

—— AFFIRMATION ——

I can summon my peace whenever I need.

DAY 90

Reflect on the Journey

We have a confession to make: From the moment you picked up this book and decided to pursue a life that looked calmer, kinder, and more joyful, you have been in your calm era. There is no "perfect" version of calm to be found. Everything you need in your pursuit of peace is already within you. You simply needed to bring intentionality into your life to activate it.

Your calm era isn't a destination you can check off on a map. Now that you've visited, you cannot simply go back to your old (anxious, stressed-out, burnt-out) life. You cannot unlearn your ability to harness your breath, calibrate your body, or practice mindfulness. These are part of you.

The journey to becoming calm is not linear. Since opening this book, you've no doubt experienced joyful, peaceful moments, as well as moments of anxiety and stress. These multitudinous experiences are part of what makes your journey so beautiful. Without the climb up the hill, we'd never get to see the view from the top. Ninety days later, and here you are. Still a glorious work in progress. Are you proud of yourself? You should be.

I am calm ✦
✦ and capable.

SEE HOW FAR YOU'VE COME

Think back on your decision to pick up this book. Think of the person you were ninety days ago. Now think about who you are today. Note five things that you do better now than you did even just a few months ago. You were always capable of growth, and you are always making progress. Celebrate the changes you see in how you respond to stress and anxiety, whether those changes are big or small.

Notes

1. Adrienne Stinson, "What Is Box Breathing?," *Medical News Today*, updated May 13, 2024, https://www.medicalnewstoday.com/articles/321805.
2. Rachel Nall, "Does the 20–20-20 Rule Prevent Eye Strain?" *Medical News Today*, updated January 11, 2024, https://www.medicalnewstoday.com/articles/321536.
3. Robert C. Barkman, "Why the Human Brain Is So Good at Detecting Patterns," *Psychology Today*, May 19, 2021, https://www.psychologytoday.com/us/blog /singular-perspective/202105/why-the-human-brain-is-so-good-detecting -patterns.
4. Kristen Fuller, "How Clutter and Mental Health Are Connected," Verywell Mind, updated August 21, 2023, https://www.verywellmind.com/decluttering-our -house-to-cleanse-our-minds-5101511.
5. Juliette Burton, "The Art of Destressing: How Creativity Creates Less Stress," Mental Health Research, April 15, 2024, https://www.mqmentalhealth.org /the-art-of-destressing-how-creativity-creates-less-stress/.
6. Shahram Heshmat, "What Is Confirmation Bias?" *Psychology Today*, April 23, 2015, https://www.psychologytoday.com/us/blog/science-of-choice/201504/what-is -confirmation-bias.
7. Mayo Clinic Staff, "Exercise and Stress: Get Moving to Manage Stress," Mayo Clinic, August 3, 2022, https://www.mayoclinic.org/healthy-lifestyle/stress -management/in-depth/exercise-and-stress/art-20044469.
8. Carole Tanzer Miller, "Walking, Jogging, Yoga Are All Good Medicine for Depression," *US News and World Report*, February 15, 2024, https://www.usnews .com/news/health-news/articles/2024-02-15/walking-jogging-yoga-are-all-good -medicine-for-depression.
9. Annie Daly, "The Real Reason Exercise Makes You Happy, According to Research on the Brain," mindbodygreen, March 3, 2020, https://www.mindbodygreen.com /articles/how-exercise-makes-you-happy.
10. Ben Kinsey, "Depression, Anxiety and Agency," Ensemble Therapy, accessed July 30, 2024, https://www.ensembletherapy.com/blog-posts/depression-anxiety -agency.
11. "Stress and Sleep," American Psychological Association, accessed September 24, 2024, https://www.apa.org/news/press/releases/stress/2013/sleep.
12. "Stress and Sleep," American Psychological Association.
13. "Newton's Laws of Motion," Glenn Research Center, NASA, accessed July 30, 2024, www1.grc.nasa.gov/beginners-guide-to-aeronautics/newtons-laws -of-motion/.
14. Joseph Wielgosz, "Change Your Posture, Change Your Mood," Happier, May 3, 2024, https://www.happierapp.com/meditationblog/change-your-posture -change-your-mood.

15. Dean Pohlman, "Mountain Pose for Beginners and Men," Man Flow Yoga, accessed July 29, 2024, https://manflowyoga.com/blog/mountain-pose-for-beginners-and-men/.
16. Kendra Cherry, "How to Stop People-Pleasing," Verywell Mind, updated May 19, 2024, https://www.verywellmind.com/how-to-stop-being-a-people-pleaser-5184412.
17. Tal Shafir, "Using Movement to Regulate Emotion: Neurophysiological Findings and Their Application in Psychotherapy," *Frontiers in Psychology* 7 (2016): 1451, https://doi.org/10.3389/fpsyg.2016.01451.
18. "Self-talk," Health Direct, updated March 2024, https://www.healthdirect.gov.au/self-talk.
19. "Health Benefits of Having a Routine," Northwestern Medicine, updated December 2022, https://www.nm.org/healthbeat/healthy-tips/health-benefits-of-having-a-routine.
20. Stefanie Veno, "Stress Relief Through Puzzles," Words About Wellness, UNC School of Medicine, accessed July 24, 2024, https://www.med.unc.edu/phyrehab/wp-content/uploads/sites/549/2020/04/4.3.2020-Wellness-v2.pdf.
21. Gina Vild, "The Benefits of Reliving Your Happy Memories: 6 Simple Techniques to Savor Your Life," *Psychology Today*, March 30, 2023, https://www.psychologytoday.com/intl/blog/a-buoyant-life/202303/the-benefits-of-reliving-your-happy-memories.
22. "Practicing Gratitude: Ways to Improve Positivity," *NIH News in Health*, National Institute of Healthy, March 2019, https://newsinhealth.nih.gov/2019/03/practicing-gratitude.
23. "Practicing Gratitude," NIH News in Health..
24. "How to Overcome the Freeze Response," National Institute for the Clinical Application of Behavioral Medicine, accessed July 29, 2024, https://www.nicabm.com/topic/freeze/.
25. Chitra Goel, "Anxiety Tunnel Vision," Axiom Medical, September 23, 2022, https://www.axiomllc.com/blog/anxiety-tunnel-vision/.
26. Goel, "Anxiety Tunnel Vision."
27. "Morning Routines for Stress Relief," Integris Health, September 26, 2022, https://integrishealth.org/resources/on-your-health/2022/september/morning-routines-for-stress-relief.
28. HealthBeat staff/Northwestern Medicine, "Health Benefits of Having a Routine," Northwestern Medicine, updated December 2022, https://www.nm.org/healthbeat/healthy-tips/health-benefits-of-having-a-routine.
29. Laura Yeager, "The Importance of Finding Your Happy Place," PsychCentral, updated April 23, 2017, https://psychcentral.com/blog/the-importance-of-finding-your-happy-place#1.
30. "NIOSH Training for Nurses on Shift Work and Long Work Hours," Centers for Disease Control, updated October 2023, https://www.cdc.gov/niosh/work-hour-training-for-nurses/default.html.
31. Jean Whitlock, Trinh Mai, Megan Call, and Jake Van Epps, "How to Practice Self-Compassion for Resilience and Well-Being," University of Utah Health, February 4, 2021, https://accelerate.uofuhealth.utah.edu/resilience/how-to-practice-self-compassion-for-resilience-and-well-being.

32. Jenna Fletcher, "How to Use the 4–7–8 Breathing for Anxiety," Medical News Today, updated on August 21, 2024, https://www.medicalnewstoday.com /articles/324417.

33. Kim Pratt, "Psychology Tools: How to Take a 'Time Out,'" HealthPsych, January 11, 2014, https://healthypsych.com/psychology-tools-how-to-take -a-time-out/.

34. Shahram Heshmat, "What Is Confirmation Bias," *Psychology Today*, April 23, 2015, https://www.psychologytoday.com/us/blog/science-of-choice /201504/what-is-confirmation-bias.

35. Melissa Madeson, "Embodiment Practices: How to Heal Through Movement," Positive Psychology, August 11, 2021, https://positivepsychology.com /embodiment-philosophy-practices/.

36. WebMD Editorial Contributors, "What to Know About Alternate-Nostril Breathing," WebMD, February 20, 2024, https://www.webmd.com/balance /what-to-know-about-alternate-nostril-breathing.

37. "Signs You Might Be Experiencing a Burnout and How to Regain Balance in Your Life," Queensland Government, Darling Downs Health, November 22, 2021, https://www.darlingdowns.health.qld.gov.au/about-us/our-stories/feature -articles/signs-you-might-be-experiencing-a-burnout-and-how-to-regain -balance-in-your-life.

38. Lisa Marshall, "Get Morning Light, Sleep Better at Night," WebMD, March 23, 2022, https://www.webmd.com/sleep-disorders/features/morning -light-better-sleep.

39. Rachel Nall, "What Are the Benefits of Sunlight?" Healthline, updated April 1, 2019, https://www.healthline.com/health/depression/benefits-sunlight.

40. Shelby House, "Anxiety Disorders: How to Stop a Panic Attack in Its Tracks," Everyday Health, updated January 16, 2024, https://www.everydayhealth.com /anxiety-disorders/how-to-stop-a-panic-attack-in-its-tracks/.

41. Mallory Creveling, "How to Tap into Your Five Senses to Find Peace and Be Present," *Shape*, updated October 31, 2022, https://www.shape.com/lifestyle /mind-and-body/five-senses-grounding-technique.

42. "Feeling Anxious? Focus on These Grounding Techniques," Englewood Health, July 13, 2020, accessed September 2024, https://www.englewoodhealth.org /feeling-anxious-focus-on-these-grounding-techniques.